THE FIRST AIR WAR

A Pictorial History
1914–1919

THE
FIRST
AIR WAR

A Pictorial History
1914–1919

TERRY C TREADWELL
&
ALAN C WOOD

Brassey's
London • Washington

First English Edition 1996

UK editorial offices: Brassey's, 33 John Street, London WC1N 2AT
UK orders: Marston Book Services, PO Box 269, Abingdon, OX14 4SD

North American orders: Brassey's Inc., PO Box 960,
Herndon, VA 22070, USA

Terry C Treadwell and Alan C Wood have asserted their moral right
to be identified as the authors of this work.

Library of Congress Cataloging in Publication Data
available

British Library Cataloguing in Publication Data
A catalogue record for this book is available from the British Library

ISBN 1 85753 122 1 Hardcover

Typeset by M Rules
Printed in Great Britain by The Bath Press, Bath

Contents

Introduction and Acknowledgements

The 1914–1918 war in the air was the first of its kind in the history of warfare. According to the politicians it would also be the last, because this would be the 'war to end all wars'. The weapons used by these young men were aeroplanes constructed of wood, metal and fabric. These flimsy, fragile flying machines carried guns and bombs into an era of warfare never before experienced by man. They offered little or no protection to the men who flew them, and even less to the enemy on the ground.

The men who took part in this aerial duelling were for the most part young and well educated, and were to die like no other had before them. A lot has been said and written about the rules of sportsmanship and gamesmanship that these young men supposedly followed, but in reality the majority fought this deadly game by the rules of war alone – kill or be killed.

The romantic side of the air war lies mainly in the minds of fiction writers and film-makers. The idea that the air battles were fought under the rules of chivalry is in the main a myth. This was a dirty war in more ways than one, as the use of gas and the fighting conditions bear testimony. The aeroplane was taken from the fairgrounds and race tracks, where hundreds of people paid to see daredevil fliers carry out aerobatics and race each other around simple circuits, to be turned into a weapon of war.

This book is about those fragile and sometimes extraordinarily named aircraft of the First World War, both fighters and bombers, and the men who flew them. The photographs will also show the precarious circumstances under which these young 'warriors' and their aircraft fought and died.

The authors are indebted to Chaz Bowyer and Jack Bruce for their unstinting advice and encouragement, and to Wendy Treadwell for reading the manuscript and checking that the grammatical construction was correct.

The time will come, when thou shalt lift thine eyes
To watch a long-drawn battle in the skies,
While aged peasants, too amazed for words,
Stare at the flying fleets of wond'rous birds.
England, so long the mistress of the sea,
Where winds and waves confess her sovereignty,
Her ancient triumphs yet on high shall bear,
And reign, the sovereign of the conquered air.

Translated from Gray's *Luna Habitabilis* (1737)

1914

The Air War Starts

On the night of 4 August 1914, the Imperial German Army attacked France and Belgium simultaneously. There had been some thought about the use of aircraft, mainly in observation roles, to keep track of enemy troop movements and transfer important military information between the front line and headquarters, but the plans for the German attack had been conceived when aviation was still considered 'a fanciful way of spending one's spare time'. It had been dismissed by the cavalry as something that just frightened the horses.

Battles were won on the ground, and towns and cities were captured by men on the ground, the role of the aeroplane did not fit into the planning of such campaigns – these were the thoughts of many of the generals on both sides at the time. Indeed, when Orville Wright had demonstrated his aircraft at Tempelhof Field in Berlin in 1909, one German general was heard to remark 'It is merely a clever circus stunt without any military value'. The following year, General Ferdinand Foch, Commandant of the *Ecole de Guerre*, witnessed a demonstration of Orville Wright's aircraft and was overheard saying 'That is a good sport, but for the Army the aeroplane has no value'. There is no doubt that both generals had cause to regret such remarks a few years later, when the aeroplane became a priceless addition to the war.

Although the French and the German military had reservations about the use of aircraft in war, the Italians had used a Blériot mono-plane, flown by Capitano Carlo Piazza, on 11 October 1911 to

A Maurice Farman 'Longhorn' outside the Aircraft Factory.

reconnoitre the Turkish lines during the Italian-Turkish war. Some weeks later the first bombs were dropped from an aircraft on the town of Ain Zara, Libya, and were to become the centre of world controversy. The Turks complained that the bombs (in reality they were only small hand grenade-type bombs) had hit a hospital; no mention was made of the huge naval bombardment of 156 shells that had pounded the town the day before, but it became the centre of significant press speculation regarding the ethics of such an act of aggression.

The British development of their air service was started on 1 April 1911 (an appropriate day in some people's opinion) with the creation of the Air Battalion of the Royal Engineers, consisting of No.1 Company and Headquarters, Airships, at Farnborough, and No.2 Company, Aeroplanes, at Larkhill, commanded by Captain J D B Fulton. At first it was only selected officers who were permitted to learn to fly and even they were not expected to make a career out of it. After a six month probationary period of training, they were placed on a four-year detachment. But then the Admiralty allowed Captain E L Gerrard, Royal Marines, and Lieutenants C R Samson, R Gregory and A M Longmore to be trained at Eastchurch, and the army followed suit.

In 1911, a man who was to have a most profound impact on the development of the Air Force arrived at the Bristol Flying School at

A balloon at the Bristol Flying School.

Brooklands. He enrolled on the course as 'Mr Henry Davidson' and paid the required £75. He was in reality Brigadier General Sir David Henderson and the reason for this subterfuge was that he did not want any special attention while he was working at the War Office. His teacher, Captain Howard Paxton, was astounded at Henderson's natural ability. He was soloing within two days and had qualified as a pilot within a week. At the time of receiving his licence from the Royal Aero Club he was 49, the oldest pilot in the world.

When it was discovered that Henderson had attained his pilot's licence, Major Hugh Trenchard decided that later he too would take the course. In the meantime the Government had decided to develop the potential of the air force for the future and a committee, headed by Colonel Seely, appointed Henderson as the Head of the Military Wing.

A Government White Paper on 12 April 1912 announced that a new service for aeronautics was to be formed. The following day saw the birth of the Royal Flying Corps (RFC), which consisted of a Naval Wing, a Military Wing, a combined flying school at Upavon, Wiltshire, and an aircraft factory at Farnborough, Hampshire. There were immediate problems because the Military Wing came under the control of the War Office, whilst the Naval Wing was under the Admiralty and neither would relinquish control to the other. Winston Churchill,

Sir David Henderson.

then First Lord of the Admiralty, asked the War Office how they intended to form an air defence of Britain. Their reply was that they had neither the machines nor the money to do so effectively. Churchill, however, through various means, acquired sufficient funds to be able to purchase aircraft for the Naval Wing from outside manufacturers, whilst the Military Wing was committed to getting its aircraft from the Royal Aircraft Factory, and had to take what was offered. Thus it was because of the petty bureaucracy that existed in the British military at the time that the Germans and the French Air Services were far better equipped than the RFC.

Also in 1912, trials were carried out at Farnborough on a variety of military aircraft being offered to the British army. They included Bleriots, an Avro-Green biplane, Bristols, Henry Farmans and BE2s. The trials and tests were exhaustive, but only to a point. The examiners could not know what the limits of the aircraft would be when they were flown under military conditions and as that situation had never arisen before there was no yardstick by which to measure them.

Winston Churchill, concerned at the possibilities of air raids, set about creating his own defence plans for the oil terminals and ports around the east and south coasts. Calshot and Eastchurch, among others, were designated as bases for the naval aeroplanes and the few RFC aircraft available were stationed at Hounslow, Middlesex, and Joyce Green, near Dartford, Kent.

Blériot Monoplane at British Military Trials.

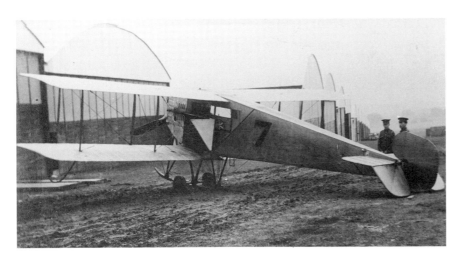

Avro Green biplane at the Military Trials at Larkhill in 1912.

A year after Brigadier General Henderson had learnt to fly, Major Hugh Trenchard arrived at the T.O.M. Sopwith Brooklands Flying School. He began his flying training on 18 July and completed it on 31 July 1912. He was then posted to the Central Flying School at Upavon, commanded at the time by Captain Godfrey Paine, RN. On his arrival Trenchard was made Adjutant, but within a year he had been promoted to Lieutenant Colonel and made second in command to Brigadier General Henderson. The Royal Flying Corps went on to attain even more independence when, in August 1913, Brigadier General Sir David Henderson was appointed Director

Staff of the Central Flying School at Upavon on 24 July 1914. Hugh Trenchard, then Assistant Commandant, is sitting third from the right.

General of the Military Aeronautics Directorate, in addition to his duties as Director of Military Training.

On 1 July 1914, the Naval Wing declared itself independent of the RFC and was replaced by the Royal Naval Air Service (RNAS). The Naval Wing of the RFC had used the *unofficial* title 'Royal' from 1912 but this became legal from 1 July 1914 with the publication of Admiralty Circular Letter CW 13964/14. To the end, in all its communiqués, the RFC called itself the Royal Flying Corps (Military Wing).

With the outbreak of war on 4 August 1914, the RFC strength of 2,073 men and women was mobilised. The majority of the drivers of staff cars, ambulances and motorcycles were women and mainly from the upper and middle classes. This was because they were the only ones who had ever had the opportunity to learn to drive, but as the war progressed, women from all walks of life were taught a variety of skills that had previously been closed to them.

Four squadrons of the RFC were immediately readied for service in France, leaving only a handful of elderly aircraft in Britain for defence and training. This contrasted greatly with the 50 or so aircraft of the RNAS that Winston Churchill had managed to 'acquire'. Fortunately the British Commander-in-Chief in France, Sir Douglas Haig, had a close understanding with his air commander, Hugh Trenchard, and allowed him a looser rein than was normally given to other commanders. This enabled Trenchard to fashion a completely different tactical flexibility from the Germans and the French, who were under strict army control.

A, B and C Flight BE2cs of the Central Flying School at Upavon in 1914.

Group of ambulance drivers of the Women's Royal Flying Corps.

In London, the defence of the capital was still a major cause for concern. It was obvious that a few aircraft would not be sufficient to repel an air attack, so Churchill reluctantly agreed to the setting up

Winston Churchill as First Lord of the Admiralty emerging after a flight.

of anti-aircraft guns around the capital. In October 1914, the Royal Naval Volunteer Reserve Anti-Aircraft (RNVR AA) Corps was formed. Because of a shortage of trained men, the Corps consisted of part-time gunners who had been recruited, on a purely voluntary basis, from City and university men and was commanded by Captain L Stansfeld, RN.

The Corps possessed just ten guns, but to make the best use of them, a retired artillery expert, Admiral Sir Percy Scott, was appointed to take charge of the AA gun defence of London. He was also given authority to develop the defence system to the best of his ability – and he did just that. Within one year the number of guns defending London had risen to 50, and in addition to this he formed the RN AA Mobile Brigade consisting of 14 lorry-mounted guns and searchlights, ready for immediate deployment and under the command of Lieutenant Commander A Rawlinson, RNVR. One of the problems facing this newly formed brigade was the variety of guns that they had been issued with: 4.7-inch, 6pdr, French 75mm and even some Russian 75mm weapons. Later these would be changed for 3-inch 20cwt AA guns on the order of the War Committee.

The airship was being used extensively by both sides and it was information about German observation aircraft from the British airship *Gamma*, that caused Lieutenant General Sir James Grierson,

Royal Naval Mobile Anti-Aircraft gun and crew ready for the road. Commander Rawlincon is seen on the left of the picture.

Commander Designate of the BEF (British Expeditionary Force) II Corps, to make the following remarks:

The Airship Gamma, *pictured in 1912.*

> The impression left on my mind is that their use has revolutionised the art of war. So long as hostile aircraft are hovering over one's troops, all movements are liable to be seen and reported, and therefore the first step in war will be to get rid of the hostile aircraft. If this is not done, warfare will be impossible unless we have mastery of the air.

Germany was in the unique position of having a fleet of long range aerial craft – 11 rigid airships. Before the war, when aircraft were only capable of making flying distances of 50–60 miles and staying aloft for about two hours, German airships were capable of staying aloft for periods of 30–40 hours and covering distances of up to 900 miles. The 11 rigid airships consisted of ten Zeppelins and one Schutte Lanz. One was under the command of the Navy, seven under the command of the Army and three civilian airships (*Hansa, Viktoria Luise* and *Sachsen*) belonged to DELAG, the German Airship Transportation Company. The civilian airships were used as training ships, after the army fleet had been reduced because of a series of accidents in which three of the Zeppelins were lost, due in the main to bad tactical use.

The first act of war in the air in the 1914–18 war was committed by the Germans on 6 August 1914, just two days after the start of hostilities. A German military airship, LZ6, commanded by Oberleutnant Kleinschmidt, dropped 420lb of artillery shells (no aerial bombs had been perfected up to this point), on the fortress of Liège in Belgium. Tactics and experience were not strong points among airship commanders and the attack was carried out at a very low altitude, bringing the LZ6 within range not only of anti-aircraft guns, but also rifle fire. Badly holed and with leaking gas bags, the LZ6 tried to make it back to her base at Cologne, but crashed in forests near Bonn where she was completely wrecked. Two weeks later the LZ7, commanded by Oberleutnant Jacobi, carried out a reconnaissance flight over the Alsace border. Emerging from low cloud at about 2,000 feet, the airship was immediately fired on by French soldiers. Within minutes she was losing gas so badly that she had to force-land near St Quirin in Lorraine and was destroyed On the same day, the LZ8, under the command of Hauptmann Andree, was on a reconnaissance flight and was fired upon by German troops followed quickly by French troops. So full of holes was the airship, that when she came down between the two forces in woods near Badonvillers, she had lost so much gas that there was not enough left to set her on fire.

The loss of these airships caused the German High Command to bring in the civilian airship *Sachsen*, as a replacement for the LZ6. Under the command of Oberleutnant zur See Lehmann, the *Sachsen* left Cologne on 2 September carrying 2,000lb of bombs. On this cloudy night the *Sachsen* attacked and bombed Antwerp, damaging a hospital and causing a number of civilian casualties before returning safely to Cologne. Many other raids were carried out on the Eastern Front against Russia, with a varying degree of success.

In England, the possibility of the Zeppelin being used for bombing missions against the British was a cause of great concern. It was thought that the Germans might justly claim that London was the centre of the war HQ and hence a 'legitimate' target. Winston Churchill

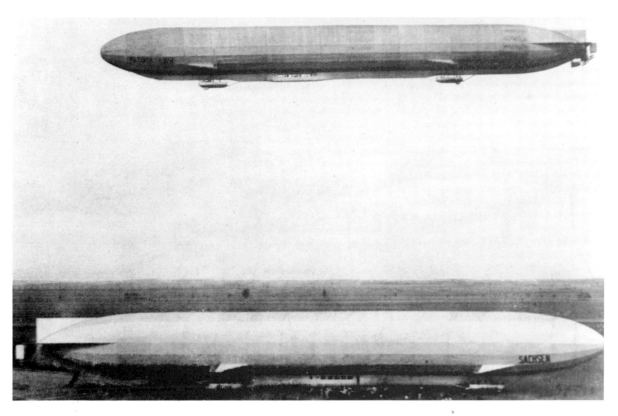

decided to pre-empt any possible German attack, by sending British aircraft to bomb the Zeppelin sheds at Düsseldorf.

On 22 September 1914, four Sopwith Tabloids of the Royal Naval Air Service, took off from Antwerp to bomb the Zeppelin sheds at Düsseldorf. Through a series of misfortunes only one aircraft got through and, despite sustaining heavy damage from anti-aircraft fire, the pilot managed to bomb one of the hangars, but the bomb did not explode. On 9 October, two Tabloids, flown by Commander Spenser Grey and Flight Lieutenant Marix, took off on a second mission to drop bombs on Cologne and Düsseldorf. Grey, whose primary target was Cologne, found that the sheds there were obscured by fog, so settled for bombing the railway station at Cologne instead. Marix, however, flew directly to Düsseldorf without incident and headed straight for the giant hangars that housed the Zeppelins. He dived, then pulled up at 600 feet and released two 20lb bombs. He watched the roof collapse, a sheet of flame shot several hundred feet into the air and clouds of smoke billowed from the collapsing structure. Inside

Two of Germany's Zeppelins, Victoria Louise (top) and Sachsen.

Squadron Commander Spencer Grey.

the brand new LZ9 was totally destroyed. Although badly damaged by ground fire he managed to nurse his aircraft back towards his airfield. Some 15 miles from home the aircraft ran out of fuel, so selecting a large field he carefully landed. Persuading a local peasant to lend him a bicycle and guard his aircraft, he cycled his way back to base.

The partial success of the mission prompted the British to make another attack on the Zeppelin sheds, this time at the Zeppelin plant

Flight Lieutenant Reginald Marix.

The only known potograph of the three Avro 504s preparing to take off from Belfort Airfield, France on the 205-mile round trip to bomb the Zeppelin sheds at Friedrichshafen.

at Friedrichshafen on Lake Constance. The long flight to Lake Constance over the Vosges Mountains had to be carefully planned so as not to violate Swiss neutrality. Four Avro 504As were secretly shipped, still in their crates, straight from the factory to Belfort in eastern France. All four were scheduled to make the flight, but on take-off only three made it, the fourth breaking a tailskid and being forced to abandon the mission. It was decided to carry on with just the three flown by Squadron Commander E S Briggs, Flight Commander J T Babington and Flight Lieutenant S V Sippe.

Flight Lieutenant Sippe in his report states that he descended to just 10 feet above the water of Lake Constance, the intention being

Babbington and Sippe being decorated for their part in the Friedrichshafen raid.

Zeppelin airship on a training exercise over Lake Constance.

that it would be less likely that he would be spotted. After hugging the north shore for five miles he climbed to 1,200 feet, whereupon anti-aircraft fire burst around him. He saw the silvery coloured Zeppelin sheds and dived to 700 feet. His first bomb was dropped to put the gunners off, the following two were dropped on top of the shed, but the fourth failed to release. The shed exploded with a tremendous ferocity. The carnage of blazing fuel tanks and burning sheds was witnessed by Babington, who had followed Sippe in the attack. Squadron Commander Briggs was shot down and injured, and hospitalised as a prisoner of war.

The Germans were shocked and dumbfounded by the attack; they could not believe that an enemy aircraft could make a round trip of some 250 miles and carry out such a deep penetration of German territory unopposed. Although they played down the amount of damage inflicted upon the Zeppelin sheds, reports from Switzerland stated that considerable damage was in fact done. New measures were swiftly introduced by the Germans to prevent a similar attack happening again.

The number of aircraft available to both sides at the beginning of the war was very small. The Germans had around 250 aircraft of all shapes and sizes, the Austro-Hungarians had around 56, whilst the Russians had 190. The French had roughly 160, whilst the British could barely muster 100. Not one of the allied aircraft was equipped for war and only represented their designers' concept of what were considered to be desirable qualities for a flying machine. Nearly all the designers at the time were pilots and as such exchanged information within their own fraternities. By 1 November 1910, the Royal Aero Club had only issued 22 pilot certificates; that is to say that only 22 pilots were considered by the British authorities to be competent to handle a machine in the air. Additionally, the RNAS had about 100 aircraft, but none of these were equipped for war. Most of the RNAS aircraft were marine types or flying boats. As early as August 1914, a base was set up in Ostende, and in September one in Dunkirk, which became the main depot for the RNAS in France and Belgium. It is interesting to note that when war was officially declared, the Halberstadt plant in Germany was associated with the Bristol Works in England. In fact, the soon to be legendary German pilot Oswald Boelcke, was actually learning to fly in a Bristol aircraft at the time.

Austro-Hungarian Albatros BII on a reconnaissance flight.

Britain was not the only country to have a naval aviation wing. The Imperial Austro-Hungarian Navy had set up their section in 1909 after several of their officers had completed flying training in Britain. The aircraft, four Donnet-Leveque and two Paulhan-Curtiss flying boats, were purchased from the French. It was the Austro-Hungarians who first used aircraft at sea under war conditions, during the international blockade of the Albanian coast, when three Donnet-Leveque aircraft were attached to the Austro-Hungarian Battleship Division. They carried out reconnaissance and photographic missions along the coast from Mount Loveen to beyond the mouth of the Bojana River.

Initially, the aircraft were based on board ship, but a variety of problems forced the aircraft to be based ashore at Teodo Navy Yard in Cattaro Bay. Later a naval air training station was set up on the island of Cosada, close to the port of Pola. At the outbreak of the First World War, the Austro-Hungarians had a total of 22 seaplanes.

In England frantic preparations were being made, with volunteers clamouring to join up to fight. Those who couldn't enlist helped to build the war machines or drive ambulances. The British were totally unprepared for war: they had no military maps of France or Belgium and had to rely upon the generosity of M. Michelin, the famous tyre manufacturer, to provide them with road maps. These very elaborate maps, though ideal for the motorist, were of no real use to an aviator. But that was all that they had and as such were better than no maps at all.

Austro-Hungarian Lohner flying boat.

The French involvement in aviation went back as far as 1870, when balloons were used for observation, dropping of bombs, carrying messages and even delivering ammunition during the Prussian siege of Paris. In 1910 the Aero Club of France suggested to the French War Cabinet that aeroplanes would be extremely useful in wartime. Within a month the French Air Service was founded and a series of flight exercises involving the use of radio and the artillery were carried out during 1911. Two years later the French Naval Air Service was formed and over 130 aircraft, mainly Nieuports and Caudrons, were supplied. With the onset of war, the French military had in total around 160 aircraft available and about 200 pilots to fly them. There were also a number of French aircraft and engine manufacturers springing up around Europe.

The French-designed Gnome aircraft engine was the most widely used at the time in France, England and Germany. At the outbreak

BE2cs under construction at the Daimler Works.

of war, the Gnome plant in Germany was seized and became the Oberursel plant. It was there that nearly all the engines for the Imperial German Air Force were built. There were also more French-built aircraft flying in England at the time than British ones, but the French aircraft were noticeably much slower. So much so, in fact, that Colonel F H Sykes of the Royal Flying Corps requested that the Henry Farman aircraft, currently in use with the RFC and a notably slow machine, be replaced by the British BE aircraft. The Director General of Military Aeronautics rejected this request on the grounds that 'the requirements of a good reconnaissance and observation aircraft demand that it should be a slow rather than fast machine'. No mention was made of the fact that a slow machine was also a sitting target for ground fire.

Allied troops were constantly being alarmed by the sudden appearance of German observation aircraft, convinced that their arrival over them heralded a storm of artillery fire of unerring accuracy. At that moment in time, however, nothing was further from the truth. The German observers carried out their task with clinical precision, but fortunately for the British the German High Command did not seem able to use the information.

An indication as to the low regard in which aircraft and their pilots

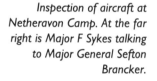

Inspection of aircraft at Netheravon Camp. At the far right is Major F Sykes talking to Major General Sefton Brancker.

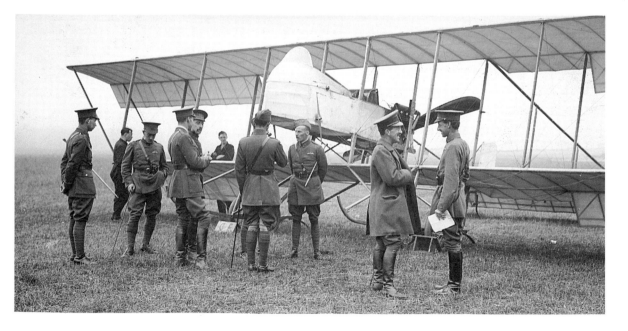

were held at the time was evident in an order issued to German officers. They were ordered to wear their swords or sabres in the cockpit
when on scouting missions. This order caused a great number of
problems for the unfortunate pilots, not only to them personally but
to the fabric of the aircraft. The order was quickly rescinded after a
number of incidents. Fortunately the British and French high com-
mands had more regard to the fragile nature of the construction of
the aircraft. Their only requirements concerned the carrying of field
glasses, a spare pair of goggles, a roll of tools, a water bottle contain-
ing boiled water, a small stove, biscuits, cold meat, a piece of chocolate
and soup-making material. Truly economy class flying of today.

In Germany there was a certain social attitude towards flying aircraft in the early years. Prior to 1914, gentlemen of means employed
chauffeurs to drive their cars and the piloting of an aircraft was
regarded in the same manner. The first pilots were drawn from the
ranks of non-commissioned officers while the commissioned officers,
usually ex-cavalrymen, acted as observers and sat in the rear cockpit.
They told the pilots where to fly and gave general instructions. One
example that epitomised this social distinction, was observed by two
British pilots during an aerial attack upon a German Albatros. They
attacked the aircraft with such ferocity that the pilot lost his nerve and
landed behind the British lines, upon which the officer observer
leapt from the aircraft, dragged the NCO pilot from his cockpit and
started to beat and kick him for his cowardice. The pilot was saved by
the intervention of British soldiers, possibly the only time he was ever
glad to see the enemy. However, it wasn't long before these frustrated
ex-cavalrymen were drawn into the excitement of the chase and
quickly grasped the chance of single combat in the air, something
denied to their brother officers on the ground.

In France, however, there was no such social barrier and the early
pilots were either ex-racing drivers or sportsmen. Again, like the
Germans, the pilots were invariably drawn from the ranks of the non-
commissioned officers, but unlike the Germans were quickly
commissioned after having proved their worth.

It was left to the French to start using the aircraft as an aerial
weapon when, whilst flying observation missions, they decided that
they could drop bags of bricks on enemy aircraft in the hope of

Sergeant Franz of VB24 with his gunner, Corporal Quennault, standing by the tail of their Voisin after shooting down the first German aircraft – an Aviatik – destroyed by a French aircraft.

smashing a hole through the wings. Later they dangled lengths of chain from above the enemy aircraft, with the intention of smashing their adversary's propeller. During the defence of Paris, the French observation pilots were ordered not to take off without taking some form of offensive missile with them, such as small bombs, hand grenades or *fléchettes* (packages of small steel arrows weighted at the tips).

The fitting of guns was the next step, but this posed weight problems. A British pilot mounted a Lewis gun on his machine which was operated by his observer. So underpowered was the aircraft, that the additional weight of a heavy machine gun prevented it climbing above 3,000 feet, while the unarmed German observation aircraft remained safely at 5,000 feet, watching with great amusement as the Allied aircraft struggled unsuccessfully to reach them. The pilot was ordered to remove the gun and resume his 'proper duties'. But he had sown the seed and with the improved aircraft came lighter machine guns. The first French aerial victory was claimed by a Voisin pilot Sergeant Franz of VB-24, on 5 November 1914. Franz, flying with a gunner by the name of Caporal Quennault who was armed with a Hotchkiss machine gun, shot down an Aviatik over Rheims.

On 11 August 1914, the first echelon of the RFC left Southampton for Amiens, France, in preparation for the arrival of the first aircraft. The first of the 37 aircraft – consisting of four squadrons, 2, 3, 4 and 5 – was a BE2a flown by Lieutenant H D Harvey-Kelly of 2 Squadron,

Aviatik BI. This was one of the earliest German two-seat reconnaissance aircraft.

which left Dover and landed near Amiens on 13 August 1914, a flight which took almost two hours. The squadron had originally left Montrose, Scotland, for Farnborough on 3 August, just hours before war was officially declared, reaching Dover on 12 August after a series of minor accidents and mishaps. The ground party had left on 8 August from Glasgow for Boulogne, arriving on the 10th.

Aircraft from 3 Squadron left Netheravon, Wiltshire, for Dover on 12 August. The start of the campaign was marred by an accident to one of the squadron pilots, Lieutenant R R Skene, and his mechanic, who became the first British airmen to be killed on active service when their Blériot crashed en route to Dover prior to flying to France. The ground crew also left on 12 August 1914, via Southampton.

The aircraft from 4 and 5 Squadrons flew from Dover, arriving in France on 15 August. It was to take a further week before all the aircraft met up with their respective squadron ground crews. This was due to a variety of incidents that covered forced landings, engine failure, minor accidents, adverse weather conditions and one pilot who made a forced landing, being arrested and imprisoned for a week as a suspected German spy.

The arrival of Brigadier General Sir David Henderson and his Headquarters at Amiens on 13 August, complete with 17 aeroplanes (nine BE2's, one BE2c, three BE8's and four crated Sopwith Tabloids) heralded the British contingent. The Royal Flying Corps with its amalgam of officers and men from all conceivable regiments and corps, together with their variety of uniforms and customs, had arrived.

The first recorded brush with the enemy that involved aircraft came on 25 August, when Lieutenant Harvey-Kelly and two other members of 2 Squadron, came upon an unarmed German Rumpler observation aircraft – also known as a *Taube* (Dove) – on a reconnaissance flight. The three unarmed British aircraft dived on the Rumpler and flew around it until the pilot was forced to land in a field. The German pilot and his observer jumped from their aircraft and sprinted for a nearby wood. Harvey-Kelly landed and searched for the crewmen but to no avail; he then set fire to the Rumpler and took off. This was the first enemy aircraft to be brought down in the First World War, albeit without firing a shot. The Germans by now had also recorded their first air casualty, Oberleutnant Reinhold Jahnow, who

Lieutenant Harvey-Kelly relaxing by a haystack after landing his BE2a in a field. This was the first British aircraft to arrive in France in 1914.

was killed on 12 August, but this was more likely due to ground fire than anything else.

The first known British casualty was on 22 August 1914, when Sergeant Major W S Jillings was wounded by rifle fire from the ground, whilst on an observation mission in a BE. There was a further recorded incident some days later, but the name of the sergeant involved was not released – probably at his own request – when a bullet fired from the ground went through his aircraft seat. A number of the British aircraft were equipped with metal seats, but not all; not long after this incident, there was a spate of thefts of stove lids from the field kitchens.

On 19 August the first air reconnaissance patrols were flown in France by the British. Three days later the first contact with the enemy was made when a patrol detected General von Kluck's II Army Corps, closing on the British front towards Mons, and was thus able to give advance warning of the impending attack.

In Germany the aircraft manufacturers were beginning to produce their brainchildren for the Imperial German Air Force. Amongst them was one of the most unusual looking aircraft of the war, the Rumpler *Eindecker*, built by the Rumpler Flugzeug-Werke GmbH., which looked more like a large bird than a fighting machine. It was originally the brainchild of an Austrian engineer, Igo Etrich, who had offered the aircraft to the German government just prior to the war. They turned down his offer, but he later sold the design to the Rumpler factory which produced a large number of the aircraft. It was one of the earliest German warplanes, and one of the best.

The early part of the war created some embarrassment and worry for pilots, especially when they were shot at by their own side. There were even instances where aircraft had landed behind their own lines, and the crews were attacked by local farmers and peasants who believed them to be enemy soldiers. Because of instances like this it was decided to paint identifying insignia on the sides of the fuselage and the wings of the aircraft. The British and French at first used Union flags; the British then introduced the roundel in December 1914 and the French in June 1915, whilst the Germans painted black pattee crosses on the wings and fuselage (Pattee being an Heraldic term depicting a cross with paw-shaped ends). As will be seen from the photographs, some of the pilots even improved on these insignia by having their own personal paint schemes on their aircraft.

As the war progressed, so did the aircraft and their usefulness.

Rumpler Eindecker.

Airmen returning after a scouting mission over the enemy lines, seen here being debriefed by the squadron intelligence officer.

Field Marshal Sir John French, the British Commander-in-Chief, recognised this when his expeditionary force was in danger of being encircled at Mons. The first four British squadrons to land in France were involved in the retreat from Mons within two weeks of arriving. It was information supplied by the RFC on German troop movements and other evidence pointing towards an attack that enabled the British and French forces to retreat with minimal loss of life.

The squadrons flew from makeshift landing fields at Le Cateau, St. Quentin, La Fère, Compiègne, Senlis, Juilly, Serris, Touquin, Melun, Coulommiers and Fère-en-Tardenois. When they took off on a mission, the pilots never knew whether the airfield facilities would still be there or have been moved by the time they got back. When they could, the pilots slept under the wings of their aircraft, and the ground crews, who had to retreat with the ground forces, performed near-miracles in keeping the ostensibly peacetime aircraft serviceable under battle conditions. In a dispatch back to the War Office in England, Sir John French acknowledged their contribution by saying:

> I wish in particular to bring to your notice the admirable work done by the Royal Flying Corps. Their skill, energy and perseverance have been beyond all praise. They have furnished me with the most complete and accurate information which has

Photograph showing the value of the observation aircraft. This shot was taken from about 1000 feet over the German lines on the Alsace-Lorraine border.

been of incalculable value in the conduct of the operation. Fired at constantly both by friend and foe, and not hesitating to fly in every kind of weather, they have remained undaunted throughout. Further, by actually fighting in the air, they have succeeded in destroying five of the enemy's machines.

There was the odd tragic incident involving the Royal Flying Corps at this time. One of the RFC pilots, who was flying low over the trenches practising signalling and the dropping of Very lights, was fired upon by British soldiers. They had been watching him and decided that he was 'behaving in a suspicious manner' and opened fire. His aircraft was hit several times and amid cheers from the soldiers, crashed into the ground. The cheers stopped when the pilot was removed from the cockpit, dead, and it was discovered that he was British. Fortunately these incidents were rare, but it did highlight the gap in communication and understanding between the RFC and the Army.

The only other country to offer any kind of challenge to the Imperial German Army was Russia. On 1 August 1914, Germany declared war on Russia and almost immediately Igor Sikorsky (better known much later for his work on helicopters) produced an improved four-engined biplane bomber, the *Ilya Mourometz* to supplement the two already in existence. The aircraft had tremendous range and could carry considerable weight, but because of the lack

Russian Sikorsky Ilya Murometz *Type B, with extended nose and deeper cabin.*

of an aero-engine industry in Russia, spare parts were virtually non-existent. Despite these shortcomings, the bomber made hundreds of successful bombing sorties and only two were ever shot down by German aircraft.

Russia also produced the first female military pilot, the Princess Eugenie Mikhailovna Shakhovska, who was posted to the 1st Field Air Squadron of the Imperial Russian Air Corps. Princess Shakhovska fought right through the First World War and survived.

The first air attacks on Britain were carried out on 21 December 1914, when a German Friedrichshafen FF29 from *See Flieger Abteilung* (Seaplane Unit No.1) based at Zeebrugge flew over Dover and dropped two 20lb bombs off Dover Pier. Some days later another FF29 dropped a bomb near Dover Castle, this being the first bomb ever to fall on the British mainland. The only damage was a few broken windows. On Christmas morning, another FF29 crossed the coast and followed the River Thames as far as Erith and dropped two bombs. Again only minor damage occurred. This time the one RFC aircraft and three RNAS aircraft followed in pursuit of the FF29, but to no avail. On the way back the FF29 was fired on by a gun at Cliffe Fort and as if to treat the whole episode with contempt, the German pilot dropped two bombs on the railway station there.

Meanwhile the same day, three British cross-channel steamers, *Engadine, Empress* and *Riviera*, converted to carry nine seaplanes, set

Ilya Murometz being loaded with bombs.

sail. These were Short aircraft, consisting of five Type 74s, two 'Folders' and two Type 135s. Their targets were the Zeppelin sheds at Cuxhaven. At 0645 hours on the morning of 25 December, flanked by anti-submarine destroyers, the three ships prepared to lower their aircraft into the water. Two aircraft failed to get off the surface of the water while the other seven, later than planned, headed south-east towards the coast. The raid was not a success, mainly because of the thick fog and the amount of fuel used by the aircraft in trying to locate their targets. Of the aircraft that took part in the raid, only that of

The converted cross-channel steamer Engadine.

Flight Commander Cecil F Kilner had any amount of measurable success. Together with his observer, Lieutenant Robert Childers, he discovered the anchorage of seven battleships and various cruisers. Combined with other information, this gave the Royal Navy detailed information on the position and strength of the German fleet. The German High Command was so disturbed by the reconnaissance flight that it immediately moved a number of big battleships into the area, damaging the battle-cruiser *Von der Tann* in the process. The aeroplane had arrived and was beginning to make its mark on the Great War.

The converted ccross-channel steamer Riviera *hoisting a Sopwith Baby floatplane aboard.*

1915

The First
Air Raids

The new year brought the war to the front door of the British. Early in January 1915, the German Kaiser sanctioned the use of airships to bomb Britain. He specified that only military targets such as shipyards and arsenals were to be attacked. In theory, this was perfectly acceptable to the German Naval Air Service, who had taken over responsibility for the raids. In reality, however, since the raids were made at night and keeping to an accurate course was extremely difficult, most of the time the commanders had very little idea of where they were.

The first airship raid on Britain took place on 19 January 1915, when two Zeppelins, L3 and L4 flying from Hamburg and Nordholz, dropped bombs on villages close to King's Lynn, Norfolk. The bombs used were mostly 110lb high explosives and 6.5lb incendiaries. Four people were killed and 16 injured. Although this number paled into insignificance when compared to the many casualties in the trenches every day, it was the first time that the civilian population had been subjected to war directly. The relative success of this mission prompted the Kaiser to sanction raids on London, Liverpool and the Tyneside area, although he did specify certain buildings that were not to be bombed. Rapid precautions were made against the threat of attack. Initially, the defence of the major cities came under the control of the Royal Navy, who converted shipboard pom-poms into anti-aircraft guns and introduced searchlights.

Zeppelin LII.

On 10 May 1915, the first airship raid on Southend took place when LZ38, under the command of Captain Linnarz of the German Army, attacked the town. Some 100 incendiary bombs were dropped, but fortunately caused very little damage. One week later at 0140, LZ38 reappeared over Margate, then headed for Dover. Fifty-three bombs were dropped, although this time LZ38 was caught in the searchlights positioned there. This was the first time that an enemy airship – in fact any enemy craft – had been caught in a searchlight, and the morale of the defence corps was boosted considerably.

May 26 saw LZ38 appearing once again over Southend, this time dropping 70 high-explosive bombs, but fortunately there were only six casualties. With his confidence high, Captain Linnarz decided that an attack on London would be his next objective. On 31 May he set out for London, appearing over Stoke Newington at 2320. Fortunately, because Linnarz navigated at around 10,000 feet, the aim of his bombers was poor and the 30 high-explosive bombs and 90 incendiary bombs caused very little damage and no casualties. What did concern the authorities, however, was the fact that this time the raider was hardly seen or heard at all, and so was able to return to base unmolested.

Up to this point, only single airship raids had been made on London. Then, on 13 October 1915, five airships, the L11, L13, L14, L15 and L16, were dispatched to carry out a raid over London. The first to arrive was L15, commanded by Leutnant Commander Breithaupt, who dropped bombs on the Strand. L15 came under very heavy anti-aircraft fire and was lit by searchlights. As usual the ground fire was completely inaccurate, but it caused the remaining airships to select targets outside the centre of London. L16, which had accompanied L15, swerved away from London and dropped its lethal cargo on the small town of Hertford.

L13 also diverted from London and bombed Woolwich and Guildford. L14 did not even reach the centre of London, but dropped its bombs on Croydon. All five airships then headed back towards Germany. The aircraft that had been based around London for its defence were launched, but failed to locate one airship. L11 which had straggled behind from the onset of the mission only got as far as Norwich, which gives a good indication of the aerial navigation skills

Zeppelin L20 in less happy circumstances.

at that time. In terms of damage and loss of life, the raid was only a partial success, but it highlighted the problems to the British of what could happen if large aircraft were to take the place of airships.

A dramatic change in the British government occurred in May 1915. Winston Churchill stepped down as First Lord of the Admiralty after the abysmal failure of the Gallipoli landings and was replaced by Arthur J Balfour. Balfour was a traditionalist and a politician, and as such, stayed with the tried and tested ways of the Admiralty. The RNAS fell under the complete control of the Admiralty hierarchy and command levels were passed to officers who had little or no experience of aviation. They moved away from the aeroplane and decided that the money would be better spent on the development of airships, as they would serve far better in a reconnaissance role. A tremendous amount was spent developing the R-series airship, not only in monetary terms but in the cost of tying up the aircraft manufacturers.

In August 1915, the *London Gazette* published the appointment of Hugh Trenchard to General Officer Commanding, Royal Flying Corps. The appointment had been approved by Field Marshal Lord Kitchener himself, after recommendations from Major General Sir David Henderson. Kitchener had watched Trenchard's rise through the ranks with great interest and had the greatest respect for him and his dedication to the Royal Flying Corps. One year later, after the RFC

Airship R-23 coming in to land. Note the converted tank in the foreground, being used as a mooring mast.

Commander Rawlinson demonstrating the new high-angle anti-aircraft gun mounting, to HRH the Grand Duke Michael of Russia and Admiral Sir Percy Scott.

had distinguished itself at the Battle of Loos, Trenchard was promoted to Brigadier General.

The Zeppelin raids over Britain were still a cause for concern, but not as much as the increasing toll on Allied shipping caused by the German U-boat. There was a growing demand for seaplanes and aeroplanes so that the RNAS could defend the ships and hunt down U-boats. The raids over Britain also served to highlight the need for a better air defence system. What was needed were better lines of communication, more powerful searchlights, better anti-aircraft guns and listening posts strategically placed around London. Experiments were even carried out by the Royal Naval Anti-Aircraft Brigade, using blind people to track the position of Zeppelins when they were out of sight above the clouds. How much success they had has never been recorded. The pom-pom guns were virtually useless and a better and more powerful gun was needed. The RNAS, at this time still in charge of the defence of London, wanted to hand over the reins to the Army so that it could concentrate on the U-boat threat. They were quite happy to continue to attack Zeppelins when over the sea, but insisted that once they were over land they should become the army's responsibility. Reluctantly, the Army agreed and the War Office took control of the defence of the cities. By the end of the war over 30 raids by Zeppelins had been made, but at tremendous cost. Of the 82 airships built by the Germans during the war, 72 of which were for the German Navy, over 60 were lost; 34 due to accidents and forced landings, the remainder being destroyed either by aircraft or anti-aircraft guns. The airship was the forerunner of the big heavy bombers that were to pound Britain later in this war and again in the Second World War.

Across the channel, in January 1915, an experiment took place with regard to using submarines as aircraft carriers. In the shelter of the Mole at Zeebrugge Harbour, a Friedrichshafen FF29 was placed athwartships on the deck of the U-12, at 0940 on 6 January 1915 and taken out to sea. About 30 miles from Zeebrugge, the bows of the U-12 were trimmed down and the Friedrichshafen FF29, piloted by Oberleutnant zur See Friedrich von Arnauld de la Perriere together with his observer Herman Mall, floated off. Despite the rough seas, the aircraft took off and headed for the Kent coast. After flying along the coast undetected, the seaplane headed back for Zeebrugge, deciding against a rendezvous with the U-12 because of deteriorating weather conditions. As far as the German Navy was concerned, the experiment was a complete success, but the German High Command thought differently and the experiment was shelved.

Wreckage of the Zeppelin LZ77, still smouldering after it had been hit by a French incendiary anti-aircraft shell.

In Egypt, the Turkish and Arab forces, who were allied with Germany, were advancing on the Suez Canal. During January 1915, British-flown Nieuport Deperdussin reconnaissance seaplanes, reaching as far as El Arish and Beersheba, revealed Turkish and Arab encampments and troops marching across the Sinai Desert. The aircraft carried out low-level bombing runs with 20lb bombs which, although not particularly effective as they were dropped into the sand, caused a great deal of panic amongst the troops. These reconnaissance flights were vitally important and were only halted because of sandstorms.

After a hectic and bloody battle lasting over two weeks, the Turkish attack was repulsed. The retreat of the Turkish and Arab armies could not be monitored from the air, because the aircraft had been grounded. This was not due to weather conditions, but simply because the engines were worn out after flying dawn to dusk operations. Helped greatly by the reconnaissance information supplied by the now worn-out seaplanes, the Allied casualties were remarkably light – 32 killed and 130 wounded. Turkish casualties,

Commander Samson in his Henry Farman about to take off with the first 500lb bomb. It was dropped on a Turkish barracks between Anzac and Kilia Liman in the Dardanelles.

including Bedouin, were estimated at 2,000, of which 716 were taken prisoner.

Whilst the battle for control of the Suez Canal had been taking place, experiments using seaplanes aboard ships had been carried out off the Dardanelles. The 7,500-ton HMS *Ark Royal* had a large number of modifications made to enable her to take on board a variety of seaplanes. *Ark Royal* was probably the first purpose-built/converted aircraft carrier. This may sound like a contradiction in terms, but so drastic were the changes during conversion that only the keel and the basic framework remained after she had been stripped, so to all intents and purposes, the *Ark Royal* was in fact redesigned and rebuilt as an aircraft carrier. She had an internal hangar for the aircraft and cranes on the port and starboard sides to lift the aircraft from the water.

On 1 February 1915, *Ark Royal* joined with the allied fleet that was preparing to force a passage off the Dardanelles. *Ark Royal*'s aircraft provided general aerial reconnaissance and spotted gunfire against Turkish forts and forces ashore. The results were useful, but because of her slow speed she became a potential target for enemy

HMS Ark Royal *showing the cranes on either side of her flight deck.*

submarines. *Ark Royal* was withdrawn and replaced by a seaplane-carrying-ship, the *Ben-My-Chree*. It was whilst operating off the Dardanelles, on 12 and 17 August, that Short aircraft carried aboard launched attacks against other ships. Flight Commander C H Edmonds, flying a Short 184 seaplane, carried out what is claimed to have been the first aerial torpedo attack against a ship. He attacked a 5,000-ton Turkish ship, suspected of carrying arms and ammunition in the Sea of Marmara, from a height of 15 feet above the water and from a range of 890 feet. Although credit for the attack was taken by the RNAS, the following day a British submarine made the same claim. Two days later, however, an attack was made against another Turkish ship using an aerial torpedo, and this time the claim was substantiated. The extent of damage caused by these aircraft has never really been determined, although there are exaggerated claims that a number of ships were sunk.

The first Victoria Cross of the war to be awarded to an airman went to Lieutenant W B Rhodes-Moorhouse, RFC, for a mission in which he bombed a railway junction. Innocuous as the mission may sound, his BE2b carried only one 100lb bomb slung between its wheels, and to make certain of hitting the target he dropped it on the railway signal box from a height of only 300 feet. The Germans had opened a four-mile gap at Ypres by the use of chlorine gas and were intending to pour troops through the gap. The only way to bring them to the front was by railway, and by destroying the signal box the advance was delayed. Not content with completing his mission, Rhodes-Moorhouse continued to circle the area obtaining German troop movements. As he flew low past a church steeple, a German machine gun opened fire, wounding him severely in the stomach, the thigh and the hand. Although in extreme pain and with great difficulty, he managed to nurse his badly shot up BE2b back to his base at Merville. He was rushed to hospital but died the following day.

The addition of the machine gun to aircraft brought it into the realms of a fighting machine. No longer the observer or 'carrier-pigeon', it was now recognised as an essential part of the war machine. One of the major problems that faced airmen was the fitting of forward-firing machine guns, which were easily the most effective weapon for air-to-air combat. Many of the Allied aircraft were of the

Lieutenant W B Rhodes-Moorhouse.

Vickers FB5 Gunbus.

'pusher' type, in which the engine and propeller were behind the crew. This gave the pilot an unobstructed view of his opponent and enabled his observer, who sat in front of the pilot, to carry out an attack without the fear of shooting themselves down. One of the first Allied aircraft to be designed for offensive missions was a two-seat biplane with a pusher engine, the Vickers FB5, or Gunbus as it was more commonly known. The first of these aircraft began to arrive at the beginning of 1915 and were issued to 5 Squadron RFC in France. However, pusher aircraft generally lacked the performance of 'tractor' types, in which the engine and propellor were mounted in front.

As usual with such problems, however, necessity became the mother of invention. A well known pre-war French aviator and stunt pilot, Roland Garros, a member of *Escadrille* MS23, realised the problems inherent in the design and designed a forward facing mounting on his own Morane Parasol (this being a tractor aircraft). He mounted a Hotchkiss machine gun directly in front of the cockpit and screwed wedges of armoured steel to the backs of each blade to deflect any bullets that did not pass between them. It was partially effective, and in the first part of April he shot down three German aircraft.

On 18 April 1915, Roland Garros was attacking the railway station at Courtrai, when his aircraft was hit by a rifle bullet fired by a German soldier by the name of Schlenstedt, which severed the fuel line and forced Garros to crash land behind German lines. That bullet was to ultimately become the instrument of one of the most important

influences on the art of aerial fighting in the First World War. Although Garros tried to destroy his aircraft he was unsuccessful, and he and his aircraft were captured. It did not take the Germans long to realise who they had captured and the prize they had in his aircraft. The wreckage of his Parasol was passed to a Hauptmann Foerster who took it to Döberitz, where a Simon Brunnhuber was ordered to make a working copy of the interruptor firing mechanism. High-ranking officers watched with great interest as the engine and propeller were set up and the machine gun was fired. It is not certain whether or not the steel of the deflecting plates was of armour-plated quality, or if the armour-piercing bullets used were of superior quality, but the propeller disintegrated and the whole test-bed was shattered. Those watching were lucky to escape without injury. It was then decided to pass the whole project over to Anthony Fokker, the Dutch aircraft designer, who, after examining the method used to fire the machine gun and recognising its limitations, decided that instead of making copies he would improve on it.

The deflector plates on the propeller of Roland Garros's Morane Parasol.

Roland Garros sitting in his Morane. The deflector plates can be clearly seen on the propeller.

A two-bladed propeller revolved at 1,200 times a minute, which meant that it passed in front of a gun muzzle 2,400 times in a minute. Fokker's design was worked by a camshaft and lever, which fired the machine gun the instant there was no blade in front of the gun barrel. The Parabellum gun fired 600 times in a minute, so his design was based on a method which made the propeller shaft fire the gun when there was no blade in the way. In all probability the actual design was conceived by another member of Fokker's design team, Heinrich Luebbe.

A Fokker Eindecker raising the dust before take-off.

However, Fokker's patent was questioned by the Swiss engineer Franz Schneider of LVG (*Luft-Verkehrs Gesellschaft*), who in July 1913 had patented a synchronised machine gun with an interrupter mechanism. Schneider claimed that Fokker's patent was based on his design, but Fokker maintained that Schneider's design was based on the blocking of the machine gun when a propeller blade was in front of the barrel.

Oswald Boelcke.

Fokker and his engineers, Luebbe, Leimberger and Heber got to work and within 72 hours they had designed and built the mechanism. Every time the propeller blade lined up with the muzzle in front of the firing machine gun, a cam, actuated by the engine, stopped the gun firing. The system was tested and fitted to a Fokker M 5K monoplane for final testing. A young Leutnant, Oswald Boelcke, was assigned to carry out the testing and after normal tests took it on a mission. After the third mission Boelcke had scored a victory (the first M 5K victory having been scored by a Leutnant Wintgens on 1 July 1915). The Germans were delighted and ordered not only the interrupter firing gear system, but the Fokker M 5K aircraft, redesignated the E I (for *Eindecker* – monoplane), as well. With the arrival of the Fokker *Eindecker* and its interrupter firing mechanism, came a new threat to the Allies. By the end of the summer, the German pilots were attacking the British and French aircraft with devastating results. They had acquired air supremacy.

Fokker at this time came under a great deal of criticism not only from his own countrymen, but from the Allies as well about his close ties with Germany. Fokker's defence was that at the onset of the war, his aircraft had been requisitioned by the German Army, together with all the spare engines and equipment. He claimed that while he was blamed for not placing himself at the disposal of the Allies, his own country, Holland, had preferred to buy French aircraft and England and Italy never even bothered to respond to his proposals. Russia was so corrupt that it would have been impossible to deal with them and the only country to express even a limited interest had been Germany. It is said that the British Government later offered him a substantial sum of money to work for them.

The French had taken possession of a number of Morane monoplanes, which had the engine in front of the pilot. The aircraft was a

Major Lanoe Hawker
VC DSO.

fast and very manoeuvrable little fighter and had a machine gun mounted in such a position that it fired over the arc of the propeller. Although a workable proposition it was very limited, inasmuch as it was difficult to aim and fire with any degree of accuracy whilst in flight.

Meanwhile on the British side, Major Lanoe Hawker, who in addition to being a fighter pilot was also a qualified engineer, worked on the problem. He, together with his mechanic, Airman E J Elton, fitted a Lewis gun to the side of his Bristol Scout. The machine gun was fitted via an attachment and mounted at an angle which, when fired, missed the propeller arc. Although very similar in idea to the French one, it was much more successful, but again it had its limitations. The modification was installed on other Bristol Scouts of 6 Squadron and accounted for a number of German aircraft in the ensuing months.

There was, however, another drawback to the Lewis gun. When the pilot had exhausted the 47 rounds that each ammunition drum held, he had to change drums. Where the Lewis gun was mounted above the top wing of the aircraft, he had to stand up in the cockpit, grip the control flying column with his knees and prise the drum off. The pilot had to hope that he could complete the operation with his opponent at a safe distance. It was hazardous to say the least. A perfect example of this occurred in May 1915, when Lieutenant Louis Strange of 6 Squadron, RFC, in his Martinsyde and during an engagement over the trenches at 8,000 feet with an Aviatik, found himself in the position of having to change the ammunition drum on his Lewis gun. As he stood up and gripped the drum, the aircraft stalled, then suddenly and inexplicably flipped over onto its back, leaving the hapless Strange hanging from the drum. The only thing that was keeping Strange from hitting the ground 8,000 feet below was the ill-fitting ammunition drum which one minute earlier he had been cursing for not coming off. As the plane started to spin down out of control, Strange managed to get hold of the centre section strut. After a series of gymnastic movements, he succeeded in getting his feet hooked into the framework of the cockpit and pulling himself back into the seat, albeit still upside down. With tremendous skill, Strange brought the inverted spinning aircraft under control, but as the aircraft righted itself, he sat down in the wicker seat with such

force that he went through the base and pieces of the seat jammed the controls. After clearing the debris he brought the aircraft under complete control and flew back to his own lines. What his opponent must have thought after observing all this is not known, but he did record seeing a British aircraft heading for the ground with the pilot hanging from it.

Observers having their Lewis guns checked by the station armourers. It is interesting to note that the armourers are Army, not RFC, at this stage.

A number of other methods of firing machine guns were tried, but in comparison with the Fokker design, they were crude. Some had Lewis guns on tripods, suspended on large awkward frameworks above the heads. One was a Lewis gun with a clamp fitted which in turn clamped on to a metal bar in the observer's cockpit. The idea was that the gun could be unclamped, then swivelled around as the enemy aircraft approached, reclamped, aimed and fired. In theory a good practical idea, in practice it was unworkable. The answer as far as Britain and France were concerned were more 'pusher' type aircraft.

The variety of makes and models of aircraft on both sides increased as the war progressed. German squadrons comprised Taubes, Albatrosses, LVGs, Aviatiks, DFWs (*Deutsche Flugzeug-Werke*) and a small number of Euler pusher models. The French had Blériots, Moranes, Henry Farmans, Maurice Farmans, Deperdussins, Bréguets, Voisins, Caudrons, REPs (Robert Esnault Pelterie) and Nieuports. The British squadrons flew BEs (Blériot Experimental), Moranes, Blériots, Henry Farmans and Avros. As can be seen, the French were by far the most prolific aircraft manufacturers of all the warring nations. The British were at a disadvantage as far as the air war was concerned: while the Germans and the French were flying and fighting over their own soil, the British were having to cross the English Channel and set up bases and fly and fight on foreign soil.

Both aircraft and air campaigns became more sophisticated as the war unfolded. Chance encounters all but disappeared and in their place came planned flights and campaigns. Tactics became the key-word amongst the various air forces, and squadron commanders became role models for the younger, inexperienced pilots. New types of aircraft began to appear, faster and more heavily armed. The French introduced the Nieuport single-seat and two-seat tractor biplanes. Both aircraft were to be the forerunners of a long and distinguished line of World War One fighters. On the other side, the German *Feldfliegerabteilungen* (Field Flying Units) were being issued with Fokker E Is with the interrupter firing mechanism, initially two

The unarmed Albatros B II, used for reconnaissance work.

to each unit to protect the two-seat observer aircraft. The arrival of the Fokker E I in large numbers proved very successful for the Germans and RFC losses rose dramatically. The FB5s of the RFC had up to this point virtually controlled the skies, but they were now outclassed and outmanoeuvred. The only respite on the horizon was the arrival of 18 Squadron. The appearance of the Fokker Eindecker dominated the latter half of 1915, but it had the effect of speeding up production of the British Royal Aircraft Factory FE (Fighter Experimental). This was a two-seat pusher with the pilot and observer in a bathtub nacelle which became a dangerous adversary to the Fokker. It halted the German domination in the air for some time, in fact until the appearance of the DH2, a single-seater pusher. This was one of the best aircraft produced by the British in World War One, but unfortunately it did not see action until well into 1916. In little more than a year, the world of aviation had gone through some of the most dramatic changes in its history. No longer did these aircraft just fly above the battles carrying out reconnaissance missions, artillery spotting and bombing – now they had to be prepared to fight for every inch of sky in which they flew. This placed urgent requirements on the aircraft designers and manufacturers of every country to come up with aircraft whose sole purpose was to fight and destroy.

Fokker Eindecker *with pilot in cockpit.*

1916

The Air War Develops

When the war first started, British and Commonwealth men and women had gone off to fight in France with a strong nationalistic pride, but, one year on, tremendous losses on each side had taken their toll on morale and the hope of an early end to the Great War appeared to be diminishing by the day. It was then that the word 'ace', created by the French, came into usage in the English language. An ace was, as far as the Allies were concerned, a fighter pilot who scored five or more aerial victories and the word had been devised by the war journalists as a method of creating heroes, at a time when morale at home was at an all-time low. Journalists and photographers of the time were drawn to the air war. It seemed that one flaming aircraft falling from a mile above the earth warranted more attention than the deaths of a hundred infantrymen.

When Roland Garros hit the headlines after shooting down his third aircraft, he was considered by the French newspapers to be an ace. It is said that an American journalist saw the story and assumed that it applied to any airman who shot down five or more enemy aircraft and mentioned it in the story he sent back to America. The British refused to accept the term and although the RFC/RNAS/RAF never sanctioned the word ace, it did officially record the combat victories in RFC Daily Communiqués and in the RFC War Diaries.

The Germans on the other hand relished the idea, but doubled the requirements to ten victories and used the word *Kanone*. Because of

Oberleutnant Max Immelmann with the wreckage of a victim at Valenciennes in 1916.

Fokker's advanced firing mechanism, the Germans had acquired a distinct advantage over the Allies and Oswald Boelcke and Max Immelmann had acquired the status of aces or *Kanonen* before 1916. They led attack squadrons whose only role was to hunt down Allied observation aircraft and destroy them. The French in particular suffered very heavy losses, so much so that the French High Command lost all faith in the Air Service reports that the occasional observation

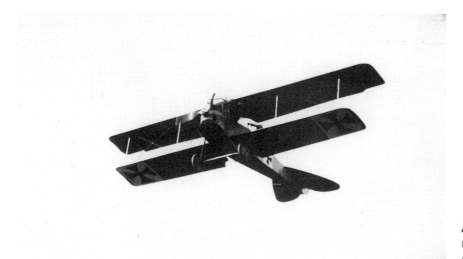

Airborne shot of an LVG CII two-seater reconnaissance aircraft in 1916.

aircraft brought back. This had a dramatic and devastating effect. During January 1915, when observation aircraft brought back information about the build-up of troops, it was ignored. 'Large scale offensives were not mounted during the worst winter months' said the Generals, but one year later, on 1 February 1916, the main German offensive – the Battle of Verdun – was launched. The information supplied by the French Air Service that should have prepared the French for this attack failed to be recognised through lack of morale, discouragement and numerical weakness.

The tide turned for the French Air Service at the end of February 1916, when, after the French ground forces had taken a terrible hammering, a counteroffensive was launched. Every aircraft that could fly took to the air, carrying bombs of all descriptions. On the ground the German forces were being pounded constantly and were continually demanding air support, but the German Air Force was either hunting for Allied observation aircraft or carrying out observation flights of its own. A slogan was coined by the German infantry that said 'Gott strafe England, Frankreich und unsere Flieger', ('God smite England, France and our own airmen'). It was to echo round the battlefields for a long time to come.

Meanwhile, a new aircraft was appearing on the scene, the French Nieuport scout plane. It did not have the synchronised machine gun of the Fokker Eindecker, but it did have a Lewis gun mounted on the upper wing controlled by a pressure button mounted on the control stick. The domination of the air by the Fokkers was over. The Nieuport replaced it as the deadliest fighter aircraft in France.

The German fighter ace Oswald Boelcke realised that the day of the Fokker was over, when he was shot down by a Nieuport of the Lafayette Escadrille (of which more later). He later submitted several reports recommending new tactics and fighter aircraft to the General Staff. The fact that he was Germany's leading fighter ace, and had written the manual on fighting tactics that was being taught to all new German pilots, lent considerable weight to his opinions. He was recalled from the front line to help reorganise the German Air Force and rewrite his tactics manual.

Hauptmann Oswald Boelcke was born in Saxony in 1891, joined the Prussian Cadet Corps in 1911 and was assigned to 3 Telegraphers

Nieuport 17.

Battalion at Koblenz. He qualified as a pilot in 1914. He flew with the *Feldfliegerabteilung* FA13, with his brother Wilhelm as observer, at the start of the war. Progressing on to single seat aircraft he started to take his toll of Allied aircraft. Awarded the Knight's Cross with Swords in November 1915 and the *Pour le Mérite* – Germany's highest decoration – in January 1916, he became one of Germany's national heroes. His report on tactical fighting in the air and submitted to the German High Command, resulted in him being given command of the fighter unit *Jagdstaffel* 2. He recruited the best pilots in the German Air Service and trained them to become the most feared of all the German units. His death in October 1916 was to be a bitter blow to the Imperial German Air Service.

The *Ordre Pour le Mérite* (Order of Merit) also known as the 'Blue Max', was originally founded by Prince Frederick in 1667 as a military decoration, being revived by Frederick II in 1740. During the First World War, the Order was Germany's highest award for individual gallantry in action. The decoration, worn round the neck from a black ribbon with white stripes interwoven with silver towards each edge, was a maltese cross in blue enamel, edged with gold and with four golden eagles between the limbs. On the upper arm of the cross was

The Ordre Pour Le Mérite
('Blue Max')

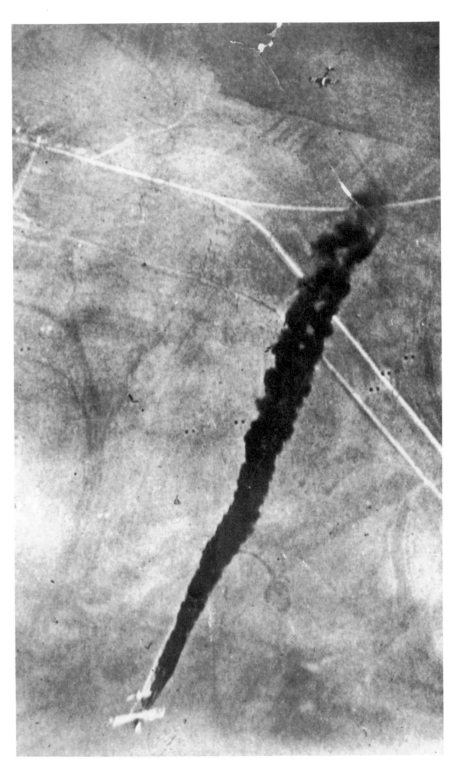

The death throes of a Voisin biplane, after being attacked by a Fokker flown by the German 'ace' Oswald Boelcke west of Verdun in April 1916 Boelcke's aircraft can be seen at the top of the picture.

the letter 'F' in gold surmounted by a crown and on the three other arms embossed *'Pour le Mérite'*. It corresponded roughly to the British equivalent of the Distinguished Service Order (DSO). Thirteen 'Blue Max' were awarded to German airmen during 1916, 28 in 1917 and 39 in 1918; a total of 80. It was not awarded after the defeat of Germany in 1918. The *Pour le Mérite* and the Iron Cross were the only two decorations awarded by Germany – each individual kingdom issued its own orders and medals.

The Zeppelin raids on London were still causing problems for the British, although only the occasional airship got through. One of the main problems for the Zeppelins was the weather. They could only be operated fully in good weather and were affected by high winds, which forced them to descend to drop their bombs, leaving them exposed to attack from the ground.

On 6 June 1915, four Zeppelins, L9, LZ37, LZ38 and LZ39 left their base at Evère, Belgium to attack England. During the flight, LZ38 developed engine trouble, was forced to return to base and was put back into her shed. The remaining three Zeppelins continued on their mission, only to find themselves in a rather thick mist. Coincidentally, at the same time, two British aircraft had taken off from an airfield in France, and were on their way to attack the Zeppelin sheds at Evère in retaliation for a previous raid on Norfolk. The two aircraft, Henry Farmans piloted by Flight Lieutenant Wilson and Flight Sub-Lieutenant Mills, arrived over the Zeppelin airfield just before dawn and circled it. The Germans on the ground thought that the engines they could hear belonged to the two other Zeppelins returning from the raid and so did not open fire on them. As dawn broke the Germans signalled to the two British aircraft with a torch and Wilson replied likewise. On seeing the huge hangars below them, Wilson dived down and dropped his four 20lb bombs directly onto the target. He was quickly followed by Mills, who did likewise. There was an almighty flash of white flame and LZ38 was no more than a mass of twisted white hot metal.

While this raid was taking place two of the other Zeppelins, LZ37 and LZ39, had given up on their raid as the fog covered a wide stretch of the North Sea, and headed back for their base. The L9 however, commanded by Heinrich Mathy, continued across the North Sea and carried out an attack on the city of Hull and the surrounding docks before returning to base. The L9 was to inflict some of the heaviest damage of the war to a British city.

As the LZ37 and LZ39 attempted to return to their base at Evère, they encountered a British aircraft, a tiny Morane Parasol, flown by Flight Sub-Lieutenant Warneford who had been dispatched from Furnes at 0100 on 7 June to intercept the raiding Zeppelins. After being airborne for only ten minutes, he was surprised to see the LZ37 over Ostend. In order to get to an altitude from which he could attack, Warneford climbed his tiny aircraft to 11,000 feet and stationed himself above the Zeppelin. He dived 7,000 feet and dropped his bombs, pulling out of his dive when only 150 feet above the target. The force of the explosion caused both craft to fall towards the ground, but Warneford managed to regain control of his aircraft and pull clear. The blast had caused some damage to the engine of his aircraft and Warneford found himself carrying out an emergency landing behind enemy lines. A quick examination revealed that the fuel line had broken, and by the light of a torch he managed to repair it with part of a cigarette holder. After considerable difficulty in starting his engine, he finally returned to base to find himself a national

Flight Sub-Lieutenant Reginald Warneford VC standing in front of his aircraft.

hero. He was awarded the Victoria Cross for being the first airman to shoot down a Zeppelin. His moment of glory was to last only ten days. Whilst collecting a new Henry Farman biplane, he and his passenger were thrown out of their cockpits during a flight and plunged to their deaths. An ignominious end for a hero.

The beginning of May 1916 saw the appearance of the Lafayette Escadrille. This combined French/American squadron, flown by volunteer pilots, was to leave its mark on the First World War and lay the foundations of an air force that was to become a world leader in later years. It had started life as *L'Escadrille Américaine*, but after protests by the German Ambassador and other pro-German groups in the United States, the name was changed to the 'Lafayette Escadrille', although its official name was *Escadrille de Chasse Nieuport* 124. It was supported and financed by many wealthy, influential Americans who believed that the United States should be actively engaged in the war as an ally of Britain and France. Initially called the Franco-American Committee, but later changed to the Lafayette Flying Corps Committee, it was headed by William K Vanderbilt, who conceived the idea of financing an American fighting unit in the French Air Service. The aim was to have American heroes in French uniforms, fighting for freedom in this new and colourful element of warfare. This, they hoped, would lend publicity to American fundraising in support of the cause.

The first commanding officer was Captain Georges Thenault and his second in command, Lieutenant de Laage de Meux. The seven original American members were Norman Prince, William Thaw, Elliot Cowdin, Victor Chapman, Kiffin Rockwell, James McConnell and Bert Hall. All their aircraft, training and uniforms were paid for out of the fund. All their mess funds were paid for and they received bonuses for virtually everything, for example the shooting down of a German aircraft brought $250 and a two-day leave in Paris. In return the committee received a source of stories and feats with which they flooded the newspapers and magazines.

One or two of the American pilots had already seen action with the French Air Force and the French Foreign Legion. The squadron was based near Luxeuil-les-Bains, high in the Vosges mountains. They were equipped with seven Nieuport fighter aircraft, powered by 80hp

One American pilot, Norman Prince, a law graduate from Harvard University, whose wealthy family had an estate in Southern France and

Some of the original members of the Lafayette Escadrille: l–r Kiffin Rockwell, Georges Thenault, Norman Prince, Alfred de Laage de Meux, Elliot Cowdin, Bert Hall (in black engineers uniform), James McConnell and Victor Chapman. William Thaw is hidden behind Thenault.

Le Rhône engines and armed with a single Lewis machine gun mounted on the top wing.

The funeral of Edmond C Genet from the Lafayette Escadrille. He was the first American to be killed in aerial combat, being shot down by ground fire whilst on patrol.

Nieuport fighter plane.

a strong association with the French people was determined to become involved in the war. He enrolled in the Burgess Flying School at Marblehead, Massachusetts, and on completion of his flying training, returned to France to enlist. Because of his flying training, his knowledge of the French language and the influential people in France, Prince was sent immediately to the Pau Aviation School, near Paris. Whilst in Paris, it is said that he used to try to persuade other Americans who lived there to join the fight against the Germans. He also tried to convince the French Air Service of the need for an American flying unit within the service and towards this end he enlisted the aid of other Americans, Frazier Curtis and Elliott Cowdin. After a great deal of argument and correspondence, they got their way. This was to be the start of the long road that was ultimately to lead to the Lafayette Escadrille.

Although Norman Prince was never an ace, he became one of Lafayette Escadrille's finest pilots and despite being credited with only two victories, left an indelible mark. His demise came at the end of one of the heaviest bomber raids of the First World War. He was returning to the airfield in the near dark when he misjudged the height of some power lines. His aircraft's landing gear caught the lines and flipped his Nieuport on its back and it crashed to the ground. Norman Prince died the following day after receiving the

Eugene Bullard.

Légion d'Honneur (Chevalier), to add to his *Croix de Guerre* and his *Médaille Militaire.*

Amongst the other Americans who joined up was a coloured American by the name of Eugene Bullard, who had transferred from the Foreign Legion's 170th Infantry. After training he qualified as a pilot and obtained a commission. He flew briefly with Spa.85 and 93, but was said to be unable to adapt to the discipline required in the French Air Service and transferred back to his regiment. Knowing the legendary discipline of the Foreign Legion, it is hard to believe that Eugene Bullard could not manage the discipline of the French Air Service and one wonders if there were other reasons. He was, after all, the only black aviator of the First World War.

The biggest problem that faced the French government was that they did not want to waste money on training men from the USA who might be withdrawn at any time. There was also a great deal of objection coming from Berlin and the German embassy in Washington, and efforts were made to try to dissuade the French from recruiting Americans and other foreigners whose countries were not involved in the war. Rumours were spread by *agents provocateurs* that these foreigners were in fact German spies masquerading as sympathisers – but to no avail, they still came.

Despite these objections, the creation of the legendary Lafayette Escadrille at Verdun gave new impetus to the French Air Service. It was a rough, tough outfit whose exploits seemed to be made of the stuff of fiction writers, which indeed some of them were. It had been created initially as a propaganda machine, whose exploits were intended to put fear into the Germans. As it turned out, it became one of the most feared of all the Allied fighter units.

In all, 180 American pilots flew with the Lafayette, and their names were inscribed on the hearts and minds of many American people for years after. Whether the propaganda campaign actually worked is a matter of opinion, as in 1916 the American people voted Woodrow Wilson into the office of President of the United States, on the slogan used by the supporters in his campaign, 'He kept us out of the war'.

Among the British aces was a young man by the name of Captain Albert Ball, VC, DSO, MC. He had enlisted in the Sherwood Foresters

Albert Ball in the cockpit of his SE5.

in 1914 when he was just 18. He paid for his own flying lessons and transferred to the Royal Flying Corps in February 1916, after obtaining his flying licence. He carried out a number of flying jobs before being assigned to 11 Squadron and allocated a Nieuport Scout. Within months he had shot down a balloon, followed by an observation aircraft. Many victims fell to his unerring accuracy with his guns and at one point he attacked five enemy aircraft whilst flying alone. Within one year he had amassed 31 'kills' and was Britain's leading fighter pilot. Not so much a master pilot, but more a master marksman.

A certain complacency had set in among the British. Confident in their supremacy over the Germans in the air, they had done nothing to improve their aircraft or their methods. On the other hand, the Germans had not only improved their aircraft, they had also created new tactics, and dominance in the air suddenly became theirs once more. In response to protests that the BE aircraft was obsolete, the Royal Aircraft Factory, who were the main producers of British aircraft, developed the RE8 (Reconnaissance Experimental 8). It was brought into service by replacing the BEs in 52 Squadron. It was obvious from the start that the RE8 was in fact inferior to any other two-seater available, and such was the initial loss rate that the squadron asked for the BE back. The RE8 continued to be built however, and was flown throughout the war by British airmen.

RE8 reconnaissance aircraft.   The realisation that a new fighter aircraft had to be built to compete with the Germans if the British wanted once again to have air supremacy, became a priority. In response the Royal Aircraft Factory refashioned the BE2c into a single-seater scout. This was not a good idea, as it had neither the manoeuvrability or the speed of the German Fokkers or Albatroses. However, there was one aircraft that fitted the bill, the Sopwith 1½ Strutter. Designed and built by the Sopwith Aircraft Company, an independent company, it was equipped with a synchronised machine gun that fired through the propeller arc. It had initially been built for the Royal Naval Air Service but was quickly brought into the service of the Royal Flying Corps because of its excellent manoeuvrability and speed. At the end of 1917, however, the best fighter available to the British was still the Nieuport – French built.

In Britain, General Hugh Trenchard, regarded by many as the father of the modern air force, saw the potential of the aeroplane as

RE8 airborne over France.

an offensive weapon and not a defensive one. On 14 January 1916, Trenchard had issued an instruction to all squadrons:

> Until the Royal Flying Corps is in possession of a machine as good as, or better than, the German Fokker, it seems that a change in policy and tactics has become necessary. In order to ensure that reconnaissance and photography patrols are allowed a fair chance of success, all fighter aircraft will raid prominent enemy aerodromes and attack any hostile machine that offers combat.

He later insisted that all combat aircraft were to fly in not less than four-aircraft formations as a form of self-protection. The day of the solo hunter and aerial duellist was over. There was a new breed of aviator in the skies, one who not only attacked, but protected his companions as well. Gone was the daredevil with his white scarf fluttering behind him as, in the words of magazine writers, 'he plunged headlong at the foe with twin guns chattering hate'. He was now replaced with the cool, calculating aviator who picked his moment to attack and only then with someone watching his tail.

New tactics were evolved, one of which was the favourite German

A British FE2b in flight.

trick of climbing as high as the aircraft would go, and, with the sun
behind them, waiting until the enemy went by, then diving down
upon them. With the sun shining into their eyes, many a pilot died
without even knowing what hit him. From this manoeuvre was coined
the phrase 'Beware the Hun in the Sun'. It became a well known tac-
tic of both German and Allied fighter pilots in the Second World War.

As the war progressed, with no sign of ending or either side giving
an inch, morale on both sides diminished daily, not only on the battlefront, but amongst the civilian population in Germany, Britain and
France. Germany decided that to boost morale, both in the trenches
and back home, they would encourage the creation of 'heroes' and
who better than the intrepid airmen who fought alone in the skies?
Among them was Max Immelmann, who, after being awarded the
Pour le Mérite, wrote to his parents: 'We were invited to dinner with the

The Albatros C III general purpose aircraft, which became the most produced of all Albatros two-seaters.

King of Bavaria, who presented us with the Orders. The King of Saxony, the Crown Prince of Prussia and Saxony, Prince Sigismund, the Chief of War Aviation and others too numerous to mention, all sent us telegrams of congratulations and already my mailbag has swelled to 50 letters a day from admirers'.

In February 1916, under constant pressure from ground commanders, the German High Command brought together a large proportion of the German Air Service in the Verdun area. It was to adopt a defensive role in an attempt to stem the counteroffensive and consisted of two bombers, 145 reconnaissance aircraft, 21 fighters, 14

Fokkers attack and destroy a kite balloon. Below the flaming balloon can be seen the parachute of the observer. In the foreground is a DFW C V.

captive balloons and three Zeppelins. There were tremendous losses on both sides, of both pilots and aircraft, but the German tactics were misguided and within weeks the command of the air in this sector had passed to the French.

Whilst the French ground forces clung desperately to the fortresses of Verdun, the British were preparing a large-scale offensive on the Somme that would take the pressure off the French and penetrate the German line. Max Immelmann knew that the British were massing troops and supplies, so it befell him and his men to supply the German High Command with accurate reports on all that was happening. Conversely, on the British side the RFC's role was to ensure that German observation aircraft never got near the British troops and an epic battle ensued.

In England, General Hugh Trenchard was shaping the RFC and creating units within the squadrons. Entire squadrons were ordered to take part in fighting attacks and bombing raids, eventually discouraging attacks by enemy aircraft. By the end of April 1916, the new tactics were producing results. The figures for the previous three months showed that the Germans had lost 42 aircraft, whilst the British had lost 32.

The Germans were forever trying to improve their aircraft, and Fokker saw to it that the aces were the first to receive the improved versions. One of them, the Fokker E III, was to be instrumental in the demise of Max Immelmann. The aircraft was powered by a twin-row, 14-cylinder Oberursel engine and fitted with twin Spandau machine guns. On 31 May 1916, Immelmann attacked a small formation of

Vickers FB9s. The 'pusher' arrangement of the engine and propellor is particularly clear.

Vickers observation aircraft. The interrupter gear on the firing mechanism malfunctioned, with the result that he shot away half of his own
propeller. The aircraft suddenly bucked all over the sky. Immelmann
switched off his engine almost immediately and eased the aircraft into
a safe landing in a field. On looking at the engine he was horrified
to see that it was hanging loose from its mountings.

One month later, Immelmann in another Fokker E III attacked two
British observation aircraft as they flew over German lines. No-one is
quite sure what happened, but one moment Immelmann was attacking the two aircraft, the next his aircraft was careering out of control.
His aircraft was hit either by the two British aircraft or by his own
ground fire, but it came apart in the air and Immelmann fell to his
death.

The generally accepted version of the incident was that in the battle with an FE, piloted by 2nd Lieutenant G R McCubbin, the
observer, Corporal J H Waller fired a burst from his Lewis machine
gun killing Immelmann instantly. A German version was that
Immelmann had been brought down by German anti-aircraft fire.
Rudolph Heinemann, an experienced German pilot who had flown
with Max Immelmann on the day, was immediately dispatched to the
area to find out what had happened. He had been told that

*The crew of a Rumpler recon-
naissance aircraft lie dead
beside their aircraft after
being brought down by French
anti-aircraft fire.*

Immelmann had been shot down, but after investigating the wreckage he realised that the official claim was wrong. Some years later when writing in the *Berliner Nachtausgabe*, he stated that Immelmann had shot away his own propeller, causing the engine to rip itself from its mountings. The remains of the aircraft were found in two parts, with half the fuselage crumpled up several hundred metres away from the main body of the remains of the aircraft.

Anthony Fokker refused to believe the report and insisted that the aircraft had been brought down tragically by German anti-aircraft fire. He was believed, but other German pilots were not so sure. The German High Command, fearful of public opinion, opted for the latter explanation. But Oswald Boelcke, a long-time critic of Fokker's interrupter firing mechanism, was forbidden to fly the Fokker again by the German High Command.

This incident brought a terrible loss of morale to the men of the German Air Service, who by now thought that their *Kanonen* were indestructible. The German Air Service was starting to suffer heavy losses, mainly due to the now superior aircraft of the Allies.

General von Falkenhayn was replaced as Chief of the German Staff by Field Marshal von Hindenburg. With the death of Max Immelmann, the German High Command had ordered Hauptmann Oswald Boelcke away from the front. He was now ordered to tour the front line units and select his own men for an aerial fighting unit. It was to be formed along the lines suggested by Boelcke in a memo he had sent to the German High Command some months earlier. At the same time a competition was held amongst German designers to create a new single-seat fighter.

All eyes were now on the Fokker D III which performed better than any other aircraft in the competition. But it had been designed around the Oberursel 160hp engine and doubts about the availability of the engine caused it to be shelved. The second choice was the Albatros D I with a Mercedes engine. With the award of the contract, the Albatros was immediately upgraded to the D II. Meanwhile, Boelcke had selected his pilots and was training them in their new squadron, *Jagdstaffel* 2. Because of a mix-up in the contracts for the new fighter, his squadron was equipped with Albatros D Is and D IIs, and Fokker D IIIs. Boelcke himself preferred the Fokker D III, despite

Albatros D I Fighter of Leutnant Büttner, photographed shortly after its capture by the British on 1 December 1916.

his criticism of the interrupter firing mechanism. He scored several victories using his own techniques before allowing any of his squadron to cross the lines. But on 17 September 1916 he was ready.

Boelcke led five of his squadron in close formation towards the British lines. On the British side, eight BEs of 12 Squadron were flying out on a bombing mission, their target the railway station at Marcoing. The BEs were escorted by six FE2bs of 11 Squadron. Boelcke commenced his attack, but they bombed the station before he could reach them. The FEs came to the rescue of the BEs, but the new training Boelcke had given his fledglings proved them to be more than a match for the British. Four FEs and two BEs were destroyed by *Jagdstaffel* 2, each member of which claimed a 'kill'. Among these new pilots was Baron Manfred von Richthofen.

In March 1916, after completing his pilot training, von Richthofen joined KG2 on the Verdun Front. Born in Breslau on 2 May 1892, Baron Manfred Freiherr von Richthofen joined the Imperial German Army as a cadet in 1909 and upon graduating was posted to the 1st Uhlan Regiment. In 1912 his regiment was sent to the Russian Front and he was attached to the 155th Infantry Division. On returning to the Western Front in May 1915, he was accepted for Air Service training as an observer. He went back to the Russian Front in July 1915 as a fully-fledged observer, before returning again to the Western Front in August to join a long distance bombing unit, with the cover name of 'Mail Carrier Pigeon Unit' at Ostend.

In August 1916, he was recruited by Oswald Boelcke to join

Manfred von Richtofen (1)
with General von Hoeppner.

Jagdstaffel 2. By the end of 1916, he had 15 'kills' to his credit and was already becoming a household name in Germany. On 12 January 1917 he received Germany's highest accolade, the *Pour le Mérite,* less than one year after completing his pilot training. Dubbed the 'Red Baron' by Allied airmen (but known as the Red Devil by his peers) and flying his distinctive all-red Fokker triplane, he continued to wreak havoc and add to his tally of 'kills'. He received every decoration that could be awarded but on 21 April 1918, his reign came to an end. He was shot down and killed whilst in action. Who killed him still remains the subject of countless arguments and stories, but he will always remain one of the most enigmatic characters of the First World War.

Another notable German pilot entered the arena during the spring of 1916, a Prussian of the old school named Hermann Göring. Born in Bavaria in 1893, the son of a former governor of German South-West Africa, Göring was not the typical military soldier. In his short career in the 112th Infantry Regiment, he was nearly court-martialled and was severely censured for disobedience before being persuaded into joining the Imperial German Air Service. After a period of time as an observer with his friend Bruno Loerzer, he became a pilot. Within a year he was amongst the aces and carving out a reputation as a fearsome and courageous fighter – a long way from the reputation he earned 30 years later.

Herman Göring in his Albatros DV.

When in July 1916 the British opened their offensive on the Somme with two million troops, the Royal Flying Corps was practically unchallenged and it was becoming increasingly obvious that the Allied aircraft had the edge. General von Bülow of the German Army wrote in his papers:

The beginning and the first few weeks of the Somme battle were marked by a complete inferiority of our own air force. The enemy's airplanes enjoyed complete freedom in carrying out distant reconnaissance.

It did not take Hugh Trenchard long to realise that he had to capitalise on the advantage that he now had in the air, and so he ordered that squadron strengths should be increased from 12 to 18 aircraft.

On 28 October 1916, the Germans lost their leading ace – Oswald Boelcke. Boelcke was leading a flight of six Albatros scouts and following him closely were two of his best pupils, Bohme and von Richthofen. Boelcke indicated that the three of them would attack two British aircraft they had spotted, whilst the remaining three Albatroses would give cover from above. As they dived towards the two British aircraft, Boelcke's aircraft collided with Bohme's and part of his wing was ripped off. Boelcke's aircraft fluttered down and crashed into the ground, killing him instantly. His funeral service in Cambrai Cathedral was attended by the staff of the German Imperial Forces and the ruling Princes of the German Empire, such was the respect in which he was held.

Britain also lost one of their aces some days later, Major Lanoe George Hawker who was shot down by Manfred von Richthofen. The aerial battle between these two aces has been regarded by many as one of the most famous of the First World War. The fight lasted more than 35 minutes and in his official report, Richthofen stated that it was the hardest fight he had ever had.

August 1916 saw the arrival of a remarkable English pilot. Edward Mannock was 34 years old and had an intense hatred of the Germans. He did not initially show much promise as a student pilot in England but his instructor, Sergeant James B McCudden, recognised a latent potential talent. In the air he was a natural pilot and an expert

Remains of a British FE2b after being shot down by a German aircraft. The body of the British pilot lies in the foreground.

marksman, but his landings left a lot to be desired. But what was remarkable, was that Mannock only had one good eye. The story goes that when he went for his medical and was asked to read the sight card, he raised his right hand and covered up his blind eye reading the card clearly. He then changed hands and simply covered up his blind eye again and re-read the card. On graduation at the end of January 1917 he was posted as a fighter pilot to 40 Squadron in France, at the same time as Lieutenant William Avery Bishop was joining 60 Squadron.

The forgotten British bombers were also in the thick of things – in fact they had been carrying out raids on the German lines for some time, but were always overshadowed by the more 'glamorous' fighter pilots. It was a bias that was to continue into the Second World War.

One particular raid carried out by eight Allied Martinsyde Elephant bombers, on the railway station at Saint-Quentin, resulted in one of the biggest explosions of the First World War. Second Lieutenant L A Wingfield attacked the station and dropped a 112lb bomb, scoring a direct hit on a train standing in the station. The blazing train was made up of 60 trucks, each loaded to capacity with heavy shells. The resulting explosion caused the whole train to detonate and almost wiped out an entire regiment of German soldiers who were waiting to entrain. Later reports stated that 180 men were killed or wounded and the damage caused to their equipment was such that

Major 'Mick' Mannock VC DSO.

William Avery 'Billy' Bishop in
the cockpit of his Nieuport.
Bishop was a Canadian who
served with the RFC.

the survivors had to be withdrawn until they could be completely
re-equipped.

Wingfield was shot down by ground fire on the way home, but
later escaped. His was the only successful strike of that particular mission. Of the eight aircraft that participated in the mission, only three
returned. Over 298 daylight bomber raids were carried out between
1 July and 17 November and over 1,800 bombs weighing a total of 300
tons were dropped. These raids were extremely effective against the
Germans during the battle of the Somme and because of Trenchard's
new tactics, they were protected in the main by British and Allied
fighters.

One such escort duty nearly saw the demise of Major L B Rees, who,
whilst on border patrol, spotted what he thought was a squadron of
British bombers returning from a raid over the German lines. He
decided to escort them back to base and turned his aircraft to meet
them. Seconds later he realised that he was amongst a squadron of
German bombers on their way to bomb the British lines. One of the
bombers left the formation and attacked his aircraft. He quickly dispatched it with a burst of machine gun fire, and then decided to
attack the formation, repeatedly diving among them despite being
wounded. The enemy aircraft turned and headed back towards their

own lines fearful that the bombs they were carrying might be hit and explode. For this courageous act Major Rees was awarded the Victoria Cross.

A 65lb bomb explodes at a railway station.

London was still coming under attack from German Zeppelins, but with improved fighter aircraft the British were now starting to take their toll of these giants. One of the best kept secrets, and also one of the most decisive weapons of the First World War, was the explosive (later known as the incendiary) bullet. It was the accumulative idea of three men, John Pomeroy, J F Buckingham and Commander F A Brock, RN (a member of the Brocks' fireworks family). Their designs were developed into one bullet that was a combination of explosives and phosphorus. When fired into the Zeppelin, it penetrated the envelope and the gas bags inside the airship, with the hydrogen that spilled out being ignited by the phosphorus. This was unquestionably the answer to the German Zeppelins and their devastating raids on Britain.

The first German aircraft raid on London was carried out on 28 November 1916, by a single LVG C IV bomber. It was a particularly daring raid inasmuch as it was carried out in broad daylight, arriving over the capital at around 12 noon. The aircraft dropped six 22lb bombs in the Brompton Road/Knightsbridge/Belgravia/Victoria Street areas of London. Only minor damage was done to buildings and only ten people were injured, but what concerned the British authorities was the fact that a German bomber had managed to fly up the Thames unnoticed and was able to return to its base safely. The early editions of the evening newspapers printed the official bulletin: 'Between 11.50 and noon this morning six bombs were dropped on London by a hostile aeroplane flying at a great height above the haze'. It was discovered later that the main targets were the Admiralty and Whitehall, but they were only secondary to the photo reconnaissance that had been carried out by the C IV of the Thames Estuary, the docks and of London itself.

Germany had lost the two great battles of the Somme and Verdun, but retained command of the air.

1917

The Battle for Air Supremacy: America Enters the War

In the February of 1917, one of the top Allied fighter pilots, a Canadian by the name of Flight Sub-Lieutenant Raymond Collishaw, was posted to 3 (Naval) Squadron at Marieux, which was equipped with Sopwith Pups. Collishaw, who only stayed with the squadron for a matter of weeks, scored two victories with the aircraft. Collishaw had started his war on anti-Zeppelin patrols early in 1916, before being posted to the Luxeuil bombing wing in France. In April, he was promoted to Flight Commander and transferred to the newly formed 10 (Naval) Squadron as Commander of B Flight, which was equipped with Sopwith Triplanes. He soon became a brilliant exponent of the Triplane, scoring four more victories to add to his tally. To distinguish his flight from the others, Collishaw had the Triplanes' engine cowlings, forward fuselage and wheel covers painted black. Each aircraft was given a white painted name beginning with 'Black' – his being 'Black Maria'. The pilots of the all-Canadian squadron – Flight Sub-Lieutenants E V Reid and G L Trapp, Flight Commander J E Sharman, and Flight Lieutenant W M Alexander followed suit with names such as 'Black Death', 'Black Prince', 'Black Sheep' and 'Black Roger'. Inevitably the flight became known as 'The Black Flight' and between May and July scored 87 victories, Collishaw himself scoring 30 'kills' which brought his tally to 38. At the end of the war his total had reached a staggering 60 victories and his decorations included the DSO and Bar, DSC and DFC. He was to reach the rank of Air Vice-Marshal in the Second World War.

Squadron Commander Raymond Collishaw in the cockpit of his Sopwith F1 Camel of 203 Squadron. Standing beside the aircraft is Lieutenant A T Wheatley.

Squadron Commander Raymond Collishaw in the cockpit of his Sopwith F1 Camel of 203 Squadron. Standing beside the aircraft is Lieutenant A T Wheatley.

The Germans noted the success of the Sopwith Triplanes and their exceptional rate of climb and manoeuvrability, and requested that Fokker produce a similar aircraft. The result was the appearance of the Fokker Dr l *Dreidecker* (Triplane) in mid 1917, but although it was as manoeuvrable, it was much slower than both the Sopwith Triplane and the SE5a. Nevertheless, Manfred von Richthofen liked the Dr l and on 2 September 1917, scored his 60th victory when he downed an RE8 during a reconnaissance flight.

On 11 February 1917, the first night bombing unit, 100 Squadron, RFC, was formed at Hingham, Norfolk. After a series of practice missions, the whole squadron moved one month later to St André aux Bois, France, flying FE2bs. Their first missions were two air raids on the night of 5 April on Douai aerodrome – home airfield of the Richthofen 'Circus'*. Four of the enemy's hangars were destroyed, but one FE2b was lost. The squadron bombed German bases behind

* The change in German tactics had created a new word in the airmen's vocabulary – '*Circus*'. This was brought about by the use of formation flying and other tactics and was to become synonymous with Manfred von Richthofen – the Red Baron.

FE2b bomber. Note the very exposed position of the observer/gunner.

the lines with FE2bs until August 1918, when it re-equipped with Handley Page 0/400 bombers and became part of the Independent Force bombing German industrial plants till the end of the war.

A new and top secret British machine gun synchronising device, known as CC gear – invented by George Constantinesco, a Romanian engineer, and developed with Major G C Colley, Royal Artillery – came into use and the squadron chosen for the first experiments was 55 Squadron flying DH4 bombers. The aircraft were equipped with this simple but extremely effective device in England and arrived in France on 6 March 1917. The results were so good that 6,000 of the devices were manufactured between March and December 1917.

French production of the British Sopwith day bombers – designated the Sopwith 1A2 and 1B2 by the French – rose and by midsummer there were 370 in service with the French Air Service on the front. In all, 4,200 were eventually built under licence and equipped with 130 hp Clerget engines. Due to their small bomb load of only 60 kg, they were allocated to the *Avion de Corps d'Armée* (Army Air Corps) instead of being used as day bombers. In addition to these aircraft, the French now had five large fighter groups in service, each with four squadrons of new Spads.

On 7 May 1917 Britain lost its top fighter ace, Captain Albert Ball. He was on patrol in his SE5 fighter, when he and other members of 56 Squadron saw and attacked two flights of *Jasta* 11. Among them was a solitary red Albatros D III, flown, it was discovered later, by Leutnant Lothar von Richthofen, brother of the famous Manfred von Richthofen. After a lengthy aerial dogfight, Lothar von Richthofen crash-landed his badly shot-up aircraft just in time to see Albert Ball's aircraft disappear into cloud. Minutes later Ball's aircraft appeared. This time it was inverted and with a thin trail of black oily smoke coming from its engine. The aircraft swept low over the German lines and crashed into woods. His body was recovered by the Germans, who later confirmed that he had died from injuries received in the crash and not in battle. He was buried with full military honours, with a number of senior German officers and Allied prisoners of war present. Albert Ball was only 20 when he died and had 43 victories to his credit. On 8 June 1917 he was awarded a posthumous Victoria Cross.

Amongst the French aces, was Capitaine René Paul Fonck, who was later to become the greatest Allied air ace of the First World War and who was a marksman *extraordinaire*. He fitted a machine gun to his

French Spad fighter. This particular aircraft, Vieux Charles, *was the personal aircraft of Georges Guynemer (see p. 100).*

(see p. 100).

56 Squadron pilots: Albert Ball is seated second from the right.

Caudron G IV and on 17 March opened his score against the enemy when he engaged five Albatroses single-handed, shooting down one and scaring the remaining four away. On 15 April he joined the *Groupe de Chasse* No.12, *Les Cigognes* (The Storks). His marksmanship was demonstrated on 3 May, when he shot down one enemy aircraft using only 20 rounds of ammunition. A few days later his score stood at four (his final total reached 75). He died in Paris on 18 June 1953.

On the British side Major Edward 'Mick' Mannock – Britain's most successful fighter pilot – was posted to 40 Squadron on 6 April 1917. Initially he was regarded as highly strung and extremely sensitive and was considered by many of the other pilots as not having the right temperament. Within a month he had scored his first victory – a balloon. Gradually he gained confidence, one month later shooting down an Albatros Scout belonging to *Jagdstaffel* 33. By the end of the year he had raised his tally to 15 confirmed 'kills', had been awarded the Military Cross and been promoted to Flight Commander.

The relatively forgotten war in the Middle East against the Turks still raged on, the fortunes of the respective air forces fluctuating backwards and forwards. One incident that stood out as particularly worthy of mention occurred in March 1917, when Lieutenant McNamara, flying a Martinsyde, was returning from a raid when he saw a BE2c, flown by Captain Rutherford, making a forced landing.

They were right over the Turkish lines but Rutherford, with a dead engine, had no choice but to land. McNamara followed him down, landed and taxied his aircraft alongside. Turkish soldiers, who were less than half a mile away started to fire. Rutherford jumped out of his crippled aircraft and leapt aboard McNamara's, but was hit in the

René Fonck.

Albatros D II scout.

leg in the process. The bullet passed right through his leg and hit the rudder bar of McNamara's aircraft. The Martinsyde never even got off the ground and crashed in its attempt. The two men were relatively unhurt and extricated themselves from the wreckage. They struggled back to Rutherford's aircraft and McNamara clambered aboard whilst Rutherford swung the propeller. As if by a miracle the engine fired and with McNamara again at the controls the aircraft took off. Although it was badly damaged by ground fire from the Turkish army, they managed to fly the BE2c back 70 miles to their aerodrome. McNamara was awarded the Victoria Cross for his part in this incredible rescue.

One of the few known examples of chivalry in the Middle East at that time was demonstrated by Leutnant Felmy of the German Air Service. After a stiff fight with a Fokker Scout flown by Leutnant Felmy, two British aircraft, piloted by Lieutenants Palmer and Floyer, were shot down. Two days later this same Fokker appeared over El Arish aerodrome and dropped a message saying that both pilots were alive and well. The message was signed by Leutnant Felmy. In a later incident two more pilots were lost over the Turkish lines when they too met up with some Fokker Scouts led by Leutnant Felmy. In the following aerial battle, Captain Brooks and Lieutenant Vautin were shot down. The next day Felmy flew low over El Arish and dropped a message saying that Brooks was dead, but Vautin was uninjured. Vautin had asked for his kit, so Lieutenant Murray Jones volunteered to drop the kit on the German aerodrome at Ramleh.

Victor and vanquished at the German airfield at Huj, Palestine. Lieutenant C H Vautin, 1 Squadron AFC (1), with Oberleutnant Georg Felmy, who shot him down on 8 July 1917.

From a height of 50 feet he dropped the kit to waving German airmen.

Five days later Felmy claimed another victim. As usual he appeared over the British aerodrome the following day and dropped a note to tell them of the fate of their colleagues, but this time he enclosed some cigarettes as a present to Lieutenant Murray Jones in admiration for his courage. The German Fokker aircraft was beginning to take its toll of the much slower and less manoeuvrable British aircraft, but the arrival in August 1917 of 111 Squadron in the Middle East flying Bristol Fighters, soon redressed the balance.

America entered the war on the side of the Allies in April 1917 and the war in Europe took on an entirely different appearence. There had been a great deal of pressure within America to join with the Allies, because of the sinking of the ocean liner, the *Lusitania,* and the unprecedented attacks on neutral shipping by German U-boats that resulted in the loss of American citizens. Up to this point it had been resisted, but on 20 January 1917 the United States of America's position was changed as a result of what is now known as the Zimmermann telegram. Arthur Zimmermann, the German Foreign

HM Queen Mary visits St Omer Depot, France, on 5 July 1917. The nearest officer is Major General Sir Hugh Trenchard who was General Officer Commanding the Royal Flying Corps at the time. The aircraft is a Bristol F2b with an RE8 in the background.

Minister, tried to keep the United States out of the war by diverting their attention to Mexico. Zimmermann sent the following coded telegram to the German Minister in Mexico:

Berlin, Jan. 19, 1917.

On the 1st of February we intend to begin submarine warfare unrestricted. In spite of this, it is our intention to endeavour to keep neutral the United States of America. If this attempt is not successful, we propose an alliance on the following basis with Mexico: That we shall make war together and together make peace. We shall give general financial support, and it is understood that Mexico is to reconquer the lost territory of New Mexico, Texas and Arizona. The details are left to you for settlement.

You are instructed to inform the President of Mexico of the above in the greatest confidence as soon as it is certain that there will be an outbreak of war with the United States, and suggest that the President of Mexico, on his own initiative, should communicate with Japan suggesting adherence at once to this plan. At the same time, offer to mediate between Germany and Japan.

Please call to the attention of the President of Mexico that the employment of ruthless submarine warfare now promises to compel England to make peace in a few months.

Zimmermann

British Intelligence intercepted the message, broke the coded telegram and passed its contents on to the Americans, who reacted angrily. On 6 April 1917 the United States of America declared war on Germany and her Allies and immediately started preparations for the war that was to follow.

In April 1917, the United States Air Service (USAS) was merely a section of the US Signal Corps with an establishment of 131 officers and 1,087 enlisted men. Out of this total there were 26 pilots. It was not until 2 June 1917 that the USAS became the Airplane Division of the Army Signal Corps. However, it was to be a further four months before they actively entered the war.

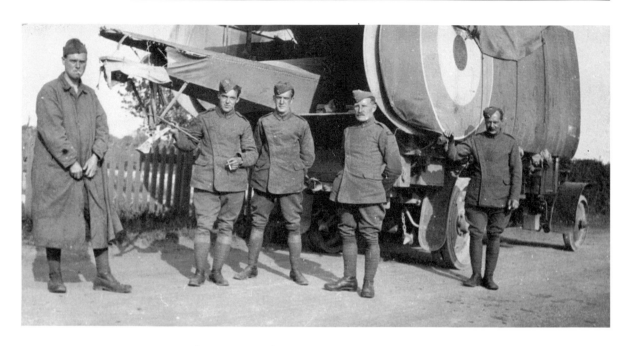

Salvage party of RFC mechanics prepare to take a crashed BE2c to their depot for possible repair on a Leyland lorry.

In France, the strength of the Royal Flying Corps at the Battle of Arras, which opened on 9 April, had risen to over 900 aircraft organised into five brigades of ten squadrons each. Each brigade comprised two aircraft wings and one kite balloon wing; another aircraft wing operated directly under the RFC (9th Wing) headquarters as a strategic reserve.

To complicate matters further for the Allies, the Russian revolution had erupted in March 1917 and the Bolsheviks began peace negotiations with Germany on 22 December. With the peace treaty signed, the Germans were then able to lay plans to stop fighting on their Eastern Front and switch resources to the Western Front against the Allies. Three million battle-hardened German and Central Powers soldiers moved from the Russian to the Western Front – this was to have grave consequences for the Allies in 1918.

The German Flying Corps had a new commander – General Ernst von Hoeppner – who adopted the policy of keeping his aircraft mostly over German lines, so that the RFC had to do battle over German-held territory. New aircraft also became operational at the time – Halberstadt and Albatros (D type) fighters: single seaters of good performance, well armed and operating in pursuit flights under good leadership in the Oswald Boelcke tradition. Large formations of

General von Hoeppner, head of the German Air Service.

'circuses' of German aircraft – sometimes 50 or 60 aircraft – were used by Baron Manfred von Richthofen to gain local air superiority over the Royal Flying Corps.

Early in April 1917, the Bristol Fighter – of which 3,101 were built – began to arrive in numbers on the Western Front and soon made its presence felt. On 8 March, 48 Squadron arrived in France equipped with Bristol F2A two-seaters and four days later 66 Squadron followed equipped with Sopwith Pups.

Bristol also produced the Bristol M1, a single-seat monoplane which had been flown at 132 mph by a company test pilot. However it had a landing speed of 49 mph which was considered too high for the small airfields of the Western Front. A production order of 125 aircraft was made and most of these were sent to the Middle East squadrons as scout replacements. A later version of the aircraft, the M1C, was used in Mesopotamia during 1917 by 72 Squadron and later by 17 and 47 Squadrons in Salonika and by 111 Squadron in Palestine.

The ground battle of Arras began on Easter Monday, 9 April 1917, in a snowstorm, but the Arras air battle had already started five days earlier. During those five days, 75 British aircraft were shot down with a loss of 102 aircrew: 19 killed, 13 wounded and 70 missing.

Among the British pilots was Captain Leefe Robinson, VC, who led a formation of six Bristol F2As over the Arras Front on 5 April, only to be met by five Albatroses from Richthofen's circus led by Manfred von Richthofen himself. The practice of flying the F2A straight and level to give the gunner a better chance of scoring hits on enemy

The Bristol M1 monoplane fighter.

Carl Schäfer, who was killed
in action on 5 June 1917, in
his Albatros D III.

Carl Schäfer, who was killed in action on 5 June 1917, in his Albatros D III.

aircraft, proved to be disastrous. Four of the F2As were shot down –
two by von Richthofen – including Leefe Robinson, who was taken
prisoner. The practice of flying the F2A straight and level was dis-
continued. Pilots started to fly the aircraft like a single-seat fighter and
suddenly the Bristol Fighter came into its own as a superb fighter.

'Bloody April', as it became known, took a terrible toll on the RFC.
At the start of the air battle, British air strength stood at 754 opera-
tional aircraft, of which 385 were single-seat fighters; the German Air
Service had 264 aircraft, of which 114 were single-seat fighters. The
RFC lost 316 aircrew during the month, out of an establishment of
700 – a casualty rate of 40 per cent. The RFC lost 151 aircraft and the
Germans 66. Many of the RFC's aircraft were lost to the Albatros
D IIIs of von Richthofen's *Jagdstaffel* 11 – Richthofen himself brought
his score to over 50 during the month.

A number of new German aircraft were now in service. The
Albatros C V, C VII, D V and D VAs could all outclass the British SE5.
The first of the Albatros D V and D VAs began reaching the Front during May. Meanwhile, the British Sopwith Camel and the DH5 were en
route to the front. The Sopwith F1 Camel – its name was derived from
the hump between the guns – was to be one of the major turning-
points for the British in the air war. Its performance and handling in
no way resembled its plodding and unpleasant animal namesake.

A DH5 fighter.

With a top speed of 118 mph, a climb rate of 10,000 feet in 10 minutes and an astonishing right turn, it proved to be one of the most deadly fighter aircraft of its time. The right turn was due to the colossal torque of its 130hp Clerget rotary engine, which enabled the Camel to carry out a 270 degree turn faster than any other aircraft could do a 90 degree turn. It took a very experienced pilot to carry out this manoeuvre with safety.

Appropriately on St George's Day, 23 April 1917, the Allied ground armies launched their second offensive on a nine-mile front at Croisilles-Gavrelle. This brought the Royal Flying Corps and the Imperial German Air Service out in strength – 68 British scouts and fighters were in the air opposed by Manfred von Richthofen's pilots, who included his brother Lothar von Richthofen. Six FEs of 18 Squadron carried out a bombing raid during the evening of 23 April, escorted by Sopwith Pups, which brought a response from two flights of Albatros and Halberstadt fighters. The resulting mêlée developed into the first large scale dogfight of the war and lasted well over an hour.

Three days later occurred one of the biggest, if not *the* biggest, aerial battle of the war. On 26 April, 94 aircraft engaged in an aerial battle that was fought at heights that varied between 5,000 and 17,000 feet. The Germans had Albatros D IIIs, D Vs and Halberstadts, whilst the

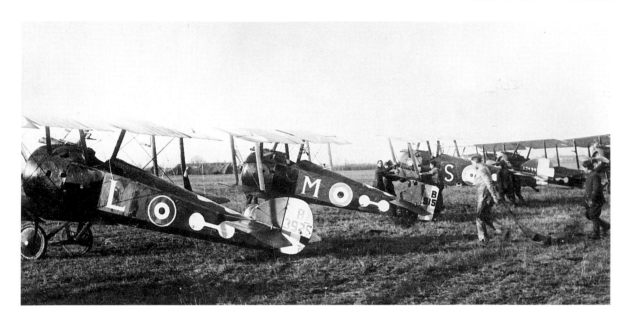

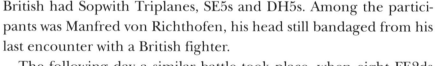

Sopwith Camels of 45 Squadron RFC.

Lieutenant Charles Nungesser.

British had Sopwith Triplanes, SE5s and DH5s. Among the participants was Manfred von Richthofen, his head still bandaged from his last encounter with a British fighter.

The following day a similar battle took place, when eight FE2ds enticed over 30 German aircraft into the area, whereupon they were pounced upon by more than 60 SE5s and 5as and Sopwith Triplanes. The British lost one aircraft, whilst the Germans lost nine. The Royal Flying Corps and the Royal Naval Air Service had fought back and the Sopwith Triplanes on 1 (Naval) Squadron and 8 (Naval) Squadron arrived and began to take their toll of the enemy. Major Roderic Dallas of 1 (Naval) Squadron, shot down eight enemy aircraft and was awarded a Bar to his DSC. Captain Robert Little of 8 (Naval) Squadron also shot down eight enemy aircraft. He was later awarded the DSO and a Bar to his DSC.

German aerial activity fell off at the end of April – 'Bloody April' was over – but the war of attrition waged by the Allies had begun to tell on the Germans.

The French pilots too were taking their toll of the enemy. Lieutenant Charles Nungesser had increased his total of victories to 22 when he shot down a German Albatros D III at Poperinghe and by the end of the summer he had increased his tally to 30.

On 20 May 1917, the RNAS made naval history when the German

Junkers J1 biplane.

submarine UC-36 was caught on the surface, attacked and sunk by an 'America' H-12 (Felixstowe F3) flying boat, piloted by Flight Sub-Lieutenant C R Morrish, RNAS.

In the same month a new German aircraft entered the war – the Junkers J1. Fitted with 5mm armoured steel plating to protect the pilot and armed with three machine guns, the J1 had been designed for ground attack and low-level reconnaissance. It was a tough and formidable adversary.

The German Albatros D V came into service during the summer, as did the Pfalz D III. The Fokker Dr I began to appear but had to be withdrawn as the top wing had a tendency to fall off. This defect was responsible for the death of Leutnant Heinrich Gonterman of *Jagdstaffel* 15, a holder of the *Pour le Mérite*, who had 39 victories. Eyewitnesses said that Gonterman was performing aerobatics in his Fokker Dr I, when parts of the top wing were seen to break away. Two

Pfalz D III. This particular aircraft was shot down on 21 December 1917 by 2nd Lieutenants Hanna and Burnand of 35 Squadron.

Fokker Dr I triplane fighter.

days later Leutnant Pastor of *Jagdstaffel* 11, crashed in a similar manner in his Fokker Dr I. Manfred von Richthofen had witnessed Pastor's accident and immediately had all remaining aircraft examined carefully. The result of the investigations sent shivers through the pilots. It became apparent that production of the aircraft had been rushed, with the result that the construction of the aircraft showed extensive examples of bad workmanship.

The crash investigation commission was summoned together with Anthony Fokker. Von Richthofen showed them the findings and insisted that the problems be rectified immediately. It was also discovered that water was getting in beneath the fabric and causing the spars to rot and the glue to disintegrate. Fokker was given a stern warning and told to improve both his production and inspection methods, and made to replace all the wings on the remaining Fokker Dr 1s free of charge.

None of these aircraft problems affected the air struggle and the Royal Flying Corps and the Royal Naval Air Service regained their strength. During the summer of 1917, the Italian Ansaldo SVA-5 – one of the finest light bombers of the war – went into production. This single-seat biplane was powered by a 220hp SPA inline engine which gave it a speed of 136 mph, comparable with the fighters of the time. It had

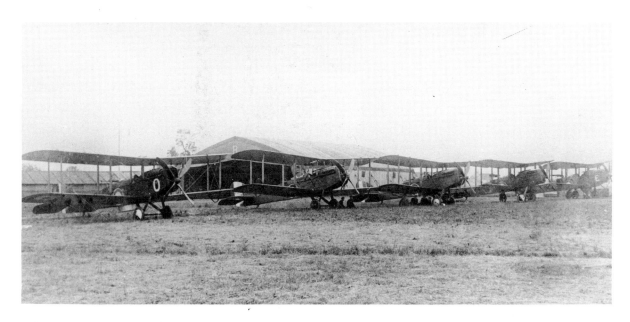

DH4 Bombers.

twin synchronised Vickers machine guns on top of the engine cowling, a range of 600 miles and could carry a 200lb bomb load. Just in service on the Western Front was the De Havilland DH4 day bomber, produced by Airco (Aircraft Manufacturing Company) and destined to become one of the best combat aircraft of the war. The two-seater tractor biplane was built almost entirely of wood and covered in fabric. The front part of the fuselage was plywood covered which gave it extra strength. When fitted with a Rolls Royce 375hp Eagle engine – which gave a maximum speed of 143 mph and an operating ceiling of 22,000 feet – the aircraft could outclass virtually all of the enemy fighters. The usual bomb load was four 112lb or two 230lb bombs carried under the lower wings and fuselage. The DH4 saw service on many Fronts – Western, Aegean, Palestine and Macedonia – and on anti-Zeppelin patrols with the RNAS.

German heavy bombers started to make their presence felt on 25 May 1917, when 21 Gotha G IVs of *Kaghol* (KG) 3, commanded by Hauptmann Ernest Brandenburg, carried out a daylight raid on Folkestone, Kent. It was the largest daylight raid of the war and 95 people were killed and 195 injured. Despite 77 British fighters being scrambled to intercept the German bombers, only one Gotha was lost.

Nineteen days later 20 Gotha G IV bombers from KG 3 struck again, this time in a daylight attack on London. Over four tons of

bombs were dropped, killing 162 people and injuring 432. Again aircraft were scrambled to intercept and again they were unsuccessful.
This led Brandenburg to think that all the targets in the southern half
of Britain were his for the taking. KG 3 struck again with 24 Gothas
on 7 July, in another daylight raid on London when 57 people were
killed. This raid, which caused a public outcry, was probably one of
the incidents that was to be instrumental in the creation of the formation of the Royal Air Force as a retaliatory weapon. On 22 July at
0800 hours, 21 Gotha G IVs crossed the Suffolk coast, turned south
and bombed Felixstowe and Harwich. In the raids, 13 people were
killed and 26 injured, but fortunately the majority of the bombs fell
into the harbour. Although 122 fighter aircraft were scrambled, only
one Gotha was brought down by a patrolling British aircraft from Bray
Dunes in France. But the day of the Gotha bomber was rapidly coming to a close. KG 3 made its last major raid on Britain on 12 August,
when 11 Gotha G IV bombers attacked Southend, Essex, and killed
32 people. Of the 139 fighters sent up to intercept them, 16 were from
61 Squadron, RFC, and one Gotha was shot down. On their return to
their base, one Gotha had to make a forced landing on a Belgian
beach and four others were wrecked on landing at their home base.

On 18 August, 28 Gotha G IVs attempted to reach England, but
were driven back by the weather. Three Gothas were lost – two to

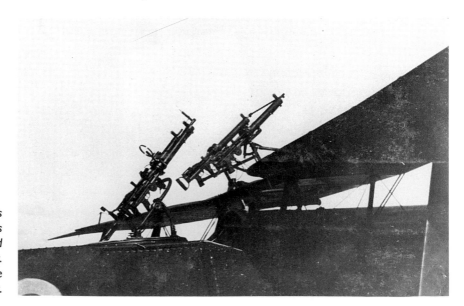

Bristol F2b with four Lewis guns' modification: twin guns in the observers position and twin guns on the top wing. This was probably a Home Defence experiment.

Dutch anti-aircraft fire and the other on landing. KG 3 was now reduced to only 15 Gothas, but on 22 August tried again. Four aircraft went unserviceable in flight and the remaining 11 reached Margate. Two more were destroyed by anti-aircraft fire and on their return were intercepted by British fighters from Dunkirk who claimed five 'kills'. The daylight Gotha bombing raids were at an end.

The German High Command decided that it would have a greater

Gotha bombers.

Wreckage of a Gotha was shot down by ground fire over Margate.

degree of success if its bombing missions were carried out at night. The British found it difficult to pick out the black-painted Gothas at night, although 44 Squadron did have some success on the early raids. In the light of these raids and public indignation, a British Cabinet Committee was formed to combat the Gotha raids. It recommended that an Air Ministry be formed to co-ordinate air warfare.

It was decided to increase the strength of the Royal Flying Corps by an additional 92 squadrons – mostly bombers. The DH4 was ordered in large batches and also a number of DH9s. However the DH9 was found to be underpowered until fitted with the American 400hp Liberty engine, whereupon it became the DH9A. The DH9 continued in service with the RFC, but suffered badly at the hands of the enemy.

Despite the orders of Hugh Trenchard that there were to be no lone missions, there were the occasional ones that captured the headlines. On 2 June Captain William 'Billy' Bishop, DSO, MC of 60 Squadron, attacked a German airfield and destroyed three Albatros D III aircraft

Gotha flying over the Belgian countryside.

which attempted to intercept him. For this attack he was awarded the Victoria Cross and his tally of enemy aircraft was raised to 25.

In Macedonia, Greece, sometimes referred to as the forgotten part of the war, Major Gilbert Murlis Green, DSO and Bar, MC and Bar of 17 Squadron had shot down seven enemy aircraft. Although compared to the number of 'kills' being scored on the Western Front such a tally did not appear to be exceptional, it has to be considered that the situation was totally different. Major Green was posted back to England to 44 (Home Defence) Squadron, flying Sopwith Camels. He was assigned to night fighting duties and on the night of 18 December 1917 he shot down his first German bomber – a Gotha G III – over the south-east of England.

The Bulgarians and Austrians opposing the British bridgehead at Salonika were assisted by German *Jagdstaffeln* 25 and 38, whose pilots included aces such as Leutnant Rudolf von Eschwege (20 victories), nicknamed 'The Eagle of the Aegean', who was the highest scoring pilot on the Eastern Front, and Leutnant Gerhard Fieseler (19 victories), who later became a famous aircraft designer.

Rudolf von Eschwege.

Attrition by the RFC continued, then on 6 July the 'Red Baron' – Manfred von Richthofen – was shot down and wounded in the head by Lieutenant A E Woodbridge of 20 Squadron in an FE2d . After hospitalisation at Courtrai and much propaganda photography, von Richthofen returned to duty on the last day of July. At an earlier incident on 5 June, Leutnant Karl Schäfer of *Jagdstaffel* 11 (30 victories) was killed, also by pilots from 20 Squadron, RFC.

Captain Arthur Coningham of 32 Squadron, flying a DH5, shot down nine of the enemy during July, bringing his total to ten victories for which he was awarded the DSO and MC. During the Second World War he rose to become Air Marshal Sir Arthur Coningham.

Belgium's premier air ace of their small but impressive *Aviation Militaire*, was Captain Willy Coppens. He fought his first single-seater Nieuport 17 air action on 21 July, but failed to score a victory. Undaunted by this, he went on to score 37 victories and the recognition of his country when they awarded him a Belgian Knighthood. The small Belgian Air Force, with only a handful of aircraft, flew with distinction – their country was occupied by the Germans which gave them more than enough reason to fight hard – 65 Belgian airmen losing their

Gerhard Fieseler.

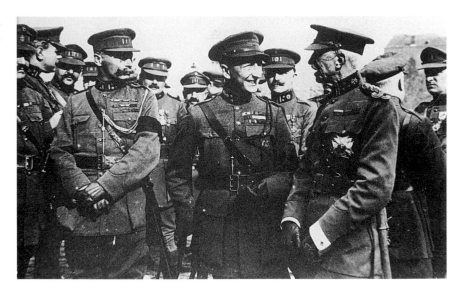

Baron Willy Coppens (centre), the top Belgian ace.

lives in the conflict. At the beginning of the war, the Belgian Air Force consisted of only 37 pilots flying Henry Farman HF20 biplanes. Their first victory was scored by Fernand Jacquet in April 1915.

June 1917 had seen the arrival of the 118 mph Sopwith Camel. It was a fighter and ground attack aircraft and was immediately in action. The Camel turned out to be the most successful fighter of the

Four members of the Belgian Air Force relaxing beside their Henry Farman HF20 biplane. The pilot sitting second on the left is Fernand Jacquet, who scored the first aerial victory for his country.

war, scoring nearly 3,000 victories over enemy aircraft. A grand total of 5,490 Sopwith Camels were built.

The RFC and the RNAS were beginning to build considerable fighting squadron strengths as follows:

Royal Flying Corps

Squadron	Airfield	Aircraft
1 Squadron	Bailleul	Nieuport 17
11 Squadron	La Bellevue	Bristol F2b
19 Squadron	Estrée Blanche	Spad VII
20 Squadron	Boisdinghem	FE2d
23 Squadron	La Lovie	Spad S VII
24 Squadron	Baizieux	DH5
29 Squadron	Poperinghe	Nieuport 17
32 Squadron	Droglandt	DH5
40 Squadron	Bruay	Nieuport 17
41 Squadron	Lealvillers	DH5
45 Squadron	St. Marie	Cappel Sopwith Camel
46 Squadron	Bruay	Sopwith Pups
48 Squadron	Bray	FE2b
54 Squadron	Leffrinckhoucke	Sopwith Pup
56 Squadron	Estrée Blanche	SE5 & 5As
60 Squadron	Le Hameau	SE5 & Nieuport 17
66 Squadron	Estrée Blanche	Sopwith Pup
70 Squadron	Estrée Blanche	Sopwith Camel

Royal Naval Air Service

1 Squadron	Bailleul	Sopwith Triplane
3 Squadron	Furnes	Sopwith Camel
4 Squadron	Bray Dunes	Sopwith Camel
6 Squadron	Bray Dunes	Sopwith Camel
8 Squadron	Mont St. Eloi	Sopwith Camels & Triplanes
9 Squadron	Leffrinckhoucke	Sopwith Camels & Triplanes
10 Squadron	Droglandt	Sopwith Triplanes

Seaplane Defence Flight based at St Pol – Sopwith Pup

Home Defence Squadrons numbered fourteen: 33, 36, 37, 38, 39, 44, 50, 51, 61, 75, 76, 77, 78 and 112.

The German Navy had conducted unrestricted submarine warfare since early in 1917, using submarine bases at Bruges and Zeebrugge. To combat this the British launched the Battle of Ypres on 31 July to capture these bases. British DH5s were used by the RFC in a ground-attack role to assist the infantry.

The United States Air Service (USAS) finally came into the European war when the 1st Aero Squadron, under the command of Major Ralph Royce, sailed from the United States aboard the SS *Lapland* on 9 August 1917. The squadron arrived at Avord at the end of the month to begin training on the ancient Nieuports the French Air Service used. Major Royce in the meantime went off to Paris to arrange further training and his place was taken by Major William O'Ryan, who, after realising that the airfield his men were destined for was not furnished or equipped, detached himself and 46 cadets for the south of Italy, to the newly completed 8th Aviation Instruction Centre at Foggia. On 3 September, Brigadier General William L Kenny was appointed the first Chief of Air Service for the American Expeditionary Forces. He was succeeded on 27 November by Brigadier B D Foulois, USAS. Then on 7 December 1917, the United States declared war on Austria-Hungary.

The arrival of the American Expeditionary Force's Aero Squadron No.1 was awaited with great interest. It had been decided by the Airplane Division of the US Army Signal Corps that 500 American pupils would be accepted into flying schools at Foggia North and

USAS aircraft at Main Field, Issoudon.

Officers of A Flight, 148th Aero Squadron, USAS. L-r: Laurence Wyly, Louis W Rabe, Field Kindley and mascot 'Fokker', W B Knox and J O 'Jess' Creech.

Foggia South. The first course was scheduled to start on 28 November 1917. Among the first American students were Allen W Bevin, later to serve with Caproni Squadriglia 13a, and Elliott W Springs, who was to join Major W A 'Billy' Bishop's 85 Squadron towards the end of the war. Another of the students, Quentin Roosevelt, the son of the 27th President of the United States , Teddy Roosevelt, had a harder time than anyone else in trying to get assigned to an air combat unit. In the autumn of 1917, he had been on duty in Paris before managing to get posted with other cadets to Issoudon. All of the cadets were in the last phase of their flying training, except Roosevelt. He had already flown at Governor's Island Aviation School, and because of this he was made a sergeant. Early in 1918, the cadets were commissioned and posted to various squadrons; Roosevelt was assigned as transportation officer and field administrator. No-one wanted the responsibility of assigning the President of the United States' son to a combat squadron. Determined to find his own way in the USAS, Roosevelt pulled all the strings he could and was eventually assigned to the 95th Squadron at Villeneuve, only to be shot down and killed on France's Bastille Day, 14 July 1918.

Another arrival from abroad who was to leave his mark upon the war was a South African by the name of Andrew Weatherby Beauchamp-Proctor. An engineering student from Cape Town, he

The seaplane carrier
Manxman.

had met a Major Miller, RFC, who was on a recruiting tour of South Africa, and volunteered to join the Royal Flying Corps. One of the things that set him apart from the other pilots was that he was only 5 feet 1 inch tall, and had to have wooden blocks fixed to the rudder bar pedals so that he could fly an aircraft. He had exceptional eyesight which gave him a distinct advantage whilst on patrol, because he was able to see enemy aircraft well before they had seen him.

Meanwhile, in England, experiments in launching shipboard RNAS fighters continued and in early 1917, two seaplane carriers – *Campania* and *Manxman* – were fitted with aircraft launching platforms. The carriers steamed into the wind and the Sopwith Pup fighters took off at full speed in a remarkably short 15 feet take-off run. The results of the experiments showed that the whole project was feasible and some 20 British cruisers were fitted with take-off platforms. Operational success came on 21 August 1917, when Zeppelin L23 was shot down near the Dutch coast by Flight Sub-Lieutenant B A Smart, who was flying a Sopwith Pup off the cruiser HMS *Yarmouth*. Smart, who had never flown off a ship before, launched himself from the forward end of the ship and at wave height sped across the sea and then climbed to an altitude of about 9,000 feet. The German observers aboard never saw the Sopwith Pup launch and minutes later Flight Sub-Lieutenant Smart hammered incendiary bullets into the Zeppelin's hull from a few hundred feet away. Smart watched the

Zeppelin turn rapidly into a fireball and plunge into the sea. He then crash-landed his aircraft beside HMS *Yarmouth*, in line with procedure, and was picked up unharmed. There were no survivors from the L23.

Squadron Commander Dunning's Sopwith Pup going over the side of HMS Furious. Crew members watch helplessly.

The battlecruiser HMS *Furious* was fitted with a flight deck and had facilities for stowing six Sopwith Pups and four seaplanes under her flight deck. In August 1917, Squadron Commander E Dunning successfully landed a Sopwith Pup on the flight deck. Some days later when he tried to repeat the experiment, Dunning's Pup was blown over the side and he was drowned.

During 1917, the RNAS began to receive Sopwith Pups to provide air protection and spotting for the British Grand Fleet to counter the German Marine Corps, who were acquiring fighting scouts to replace their seaplanes.

The strength of the French *Aéronautique Militaire* had risen from 2,263 men at the start of 1917 to 3,556 men by early August. In addition to the increased force of men, General Pétain had ordered that

The remains of Dunning's Pup on the deck of Furious *after the fatal crash.*

the strength of front-line squadrons be increased to 60 fighter squadrons with 15 aircraft each, 20 bomber squadrons with 15 aircraft each, 40 artillery-spotting squadrons with 10 aircraft each and 100 squadrons for observation and reconnaissance. In addition to these there were to be eight other special duties squadrons created.

Two more of the war's fighter aces were killed in August 1917. Oberleutnant Eduard Ritter von Dostler, holder of the *Pour le Mérite* with 26 victories, was shot down by Lieutenant M O'Callaghan and N Sharples of 7 Squadron, flying an RE8. The second was the great French air ace, Capitaine Georges Marie Ludovic Jules Guynemer, holder of the *Médaille Militaire, Légion D' Honneur (Chevalier), Légion D'Honneur (Officier), Croix de Guerre* with 26 Palms and the British DSO, of *Escadrille* N3/SPA 3. He was shot down by Leutnant Kurt Weissman of *Jagdstaffel* 3 whilst over enemy lines during aerial combat. His last resting place is unknown as the area of his grave was the target of an artillery barrage shortly after he was buried.

Four more British squadrons were sent to France in September:

Squadron	Base	Aircraft
28 Squadron	St. Omer	Sopwith Camels
64 Squadron	St. Omer	DH5
68 Squadron	Baizieux	DH5
84 Squadron	Littres	SE5a

Georges Guynemer.

The RNAS St Pol Defence Flight – defending the channel coast and providing air cover and protection for the British navy – took delivery of Sopwith Camels during September. In December it became 13 (Naval) Squadron under the command of Squadron Commander Raymond Collishaw.

Another of Germany's top fighter aces met his death in late September – Leutnant Werner Voss of *Jagdstaffel* 10. Flying his Fokker Dr I triplane, Voss had started the day well when he shot down his 48th adversary, a DH4. But later that day, whilst accompanied by an Albatros from *Jagdstaffel* 10, he engaged seven SE5a fighters from 56 Squadron, RFC. It was to be one of the most famous 'dogfights' of the First World War, as unknown to Voss, he was to cross swords with some of the top aces of the RFC. With tremendous flying skills Voss fought his opponents. He attacked the British pilots, who included James McCudden (57 victories), Arthur Rhys-Davies (25 victories), Geoffrey

Werner Voss standing in front of his Fokker Dr I with a 'totem-pole' face caricature painted on the cowling.

Bowman (32 victories), Leonard Barlow (20 victories), Robert Childlaw-Roberts (ten victories), and Keith Muspratt (eight victories), scoring hits on all of them. But at 1935 hours he fell beneath the guns of Lieutenant Rhys-Davies and crashed at Frezenburg where he was buried with military honours by British soldiers.

In the Palestine desert 67 (Australian) Squadron, equipped with Bristol F2bs, had gained air superiority over the enemy and was taking a heavy toll of their aircraft. Captain Ross Smith (later to become famous for his long-range civil flights after the war) and his observer Lieutenant E A Mustar flew a Bristol fighter throughout the campaign and destroyed 17 enemy aircraft.

A new wing was created on 11 October 1917 to carry out strategic bombing of the German industrial heartland. The 41st Wing, as it was known, was under the command of Lieutenant Colonel Cyril Newall, RFC, and its targets were Trier, Koblenz, Mainz, Frankfurt and Stuttgart. It had been calculated that these targets could be reached by the RFC from airfields around Nancy and Lorraine and destruction of them could inflict heavy damage on the German industrial economy. The Wing was very small, consisting of only three squadrons, 55 Squadron with DH4s, 100 Squadron with FE2bs and Naval A Squadron with Handley Page 0/100s.

The first daylight raid was carried out by 55 Squadron against the German steel works at Burbach, Saarbrücken. Two days later on 24 October, the first night raid was carried out by nine Handley Page 0/100s of Naval A Squadron and 14 FE2bs of 100 Squadron in atrocious weather conditions against the Burbach steel works. The raid was successful, although two Handley Page 0/100s and two FE2bs were lost. But the first long-distance raid took place on Christmas Eve 1917, when 10 DH4s of 55 Squadron bombed Mannheim and Ludwigshafen from 13,000 feet causing extensive damage. In February the following year 41st Wing was renamed VIII Brigade, Independent Force, Royal Flying Corps, under the command of Major General Sir Hugh Trenchard, and by June it had carried out a total of 142 raids on targets in Germany.

Meanwhile on the ground, the tank battle of Cambrai began on 20 November 1917. For the tanks there was no real problem, but for the Royal Flying Corps the inclement weather restricted air operations. Nine British squadrons became involved: 3, 43 and 46 who were flying Sopwith Camels, 64 and 68 Squadrons who were flying DH5s, 56, 41 and 84 flying SE5s and 11 Squadron who were flying Bristol fighters.

At first only three German *Jagdstaffels* opposed them, 5, 12 and 37, but reinforcements in the form of JG1 arrived on 23 November from Ypres. The leader of JG1 was Manfred von Richthofen and he was in action almost immediately shooting down a DH5, whilst his brother Lothar opened his account with the shooting down of a Bristol F2b.

Handley Page 0/100 in March 1917. The pilot was Squadron Commander Spenser Grey. On the right of the picture is a Sopwith Triplane, to the left a Nieuport.

SE5 fighter. This particular aircraft was shot down by Josef Mai in November 1917.

The arrival of *Jagdstaffel* 1 boosted the morale of the other three *Jagdstaffeln* and JG 5 pilots then took their toll of RFC aircraft. Leutnant Fritz Rumey shot down two Sopwith Camels and an Armstrong Whitworth FK 8; Leutnant Otto Konnecke downed another Sopwith Camel and a DH5, whilst Leutnant Josef Mai claimed a DH5, a Sopwith Camel and an F2b.

The Cambrai Allied tank and ground attack came to an abrupt halt, due in the main to the lack of reserves, and the Germans retook the ground that had been lost to the Allies' new weapon – the tank. Both armies took time to regroup, but it was obvious to all that it was going to end in stalemate.

The German *Jagdstaffeln* were still taking their toll of Allied aircraft and the reappearance of the Fokker Dr I – the problem of the collapsing wing apparently solved – did nothing to boost the morale of the Allied pilots. The Fokker was a dangerous opponent, with a top speed of 103 mph and a very high degree of manoeuvrability. But gradually the tide turned, and the number of German aces being shot down was badly affecting the morale of the people back in Germany. The German government had set these men on pedestals, to the extent that they had actually issued a series of postcards of the aces.

The announcement of the death of another of the aces, Leutnant Erwin Bohme, of *Jagdstaffel* 29, whose own aircraft had collided with the legendary Oswald Boelcke's aircraft causing his death a year

An extremely rare air-to-air photograph of an Allied aircraft going down in flames. Note the German victor above.

A Sopwith Camel of 28 Squadron in Italy.

previously, rocked the morale of the German people. Bohme met his death in air combat on 29 November when he was shot down by the crew of an FK 8 of 10 Squadron, RFC. Just five days previously he had been told of his award of the 'Blue Max', but he never lived to collect it. He was buried by the British at Keerselaarhook, his remains being exhumed after the war and returned to Germany.

Germany's ally Austria, assisted by strong German forces, attacked the Italian Second Army on the Italian Front at Caporetto, causing the Italians to retreat. Britain and France sent ground and air forces to restore the situation. Three squadrons – 28, 45 and 66 – were equipped with Sopwith Camels.

Their adversaries were at first the German Austro-Hungarian Air Service, flying Albatros (Offag) D IIIs, Aviatiks, Berg DIs, Phoenix Scouts and Brandenburg two-seaters. Amongst the pilots was one of the top Austro-Hungarian aces, Hauptmann Godwin Brumowski of Flik (*Flieger Kompanie*, or 'Flying Company') 41, flying a Brandenburg D1 and later Albatros DIIIs. He became Austria-Hungary's highest-scoring pilot with 35 victories. Flik 41 aircraft were blazoned with a white skull on a black background. Godwin Brumowski was a former

Austria's top-scoring ace, Oberleutnant Godwin Brumowski, and the personal 'skull' insignia used on his Albatros D III.

artillery officer who transferred to the Austro-Hungarian Imperial Air Service just after the start of the war.

Outstanding amongst the Allied airmen in Italy was Major Francesco Baracca of the 91st Squadriglia, flying a Spad S VII. During the desperate air fighting in the formative years, he brought his victories to 30. Major Baracca was later shot down and killed with his score at 34 victories. Also Capitane Prince Ruffo di Calabria, Tenente

Austrian Aviatak brought down intact by Italians.

Ferruccio Ranza, Tenente Luigi Olivari and Tenente Gastone Novelli accounted for a number of enemy aircraft.

The German aircraft designer Ernst Heinkel – with the aid of Oberleutnant zur See Friedrich Christiansen, Commanding Officer of the German Naval Air Station at Zeebrugge – began designing a new floatplane, the Hansa Brandenburg W29, in an effort to keep ahead of British RNAS aircraft. Christiansen later claimed as a victory the British submarine C25 which was attacked and damaged at sea. He was later awarded the *Pour le Mérite* for this and other victories.

The Vickers Vimy FB27 prototype first flew in late 1917, and so successful were the tests that the RFC ordered 150. But the aircraft arrived too late to see war service. Sopwith, too, was producing new aircraft in the shape of the Sopwith 5F1 Dolphin. It was the world's first four-gun fighter, had a climb rate of 855 feet per minute and a top speed of 131 mph. It was immediately recognisable because of its back staggered wings, and six squadrons took delivery of it late in 1917.

Following the American declaration of war on Germany in April, the United States went on to declare war against Germany's allies, Austria and Hungary, on 7 December 1917. The Germans responded by creating the *Amerikaprogramm* to counter the industrial might of the United States. The Imperial German Air Service had to be increased against the threat of American mass-produced armament. In all, 153 *Fliegerabteilungen*, 80 *Jagdstaffeln*, 38 *Schlachtstaffeln* and seven *Bombengeschwader*, totalling 24 *Staffeln*, were created.

The tide of the war in Europe and the Middle East was beginning to turn and the might of the American forces and armament factories was beginning to have a devastating effect on Germany and her Allies.

1918–1919

The Final Conclusion

On 2 January 1918, the British Air Council and Air Ministry were created. Lord Rothermere was appointed Secretary of State for Air and President of the Council, while Major General Sir Hugh Trenchard became the first Chief of the Air Staff with Rear Admiral Mark Kerr as his deputy. On 18 January, Major General Sir John Salmond succeeded Trenchard as commander of the Royal Flying Corps in France.

Three months later, on 1 April 1918, the Royal Air Force came into being as a result of the merging of the Royal Naval Air Service and the Royal Flying Corps, although naval aircraft continued to be controlled by the Admiralty. There were a number of reasons for the formation of the Royal Air Force. One of the principal reasons, was the increased demand from the public for retaliation against German air raids on Britain. In addition to this, the air side of the military was becoming increasingly larger and more important. This was starting to lead to acrimony within the Air Board, particularly at the height of the Battle of the Somme in August 1916, when the Admiralty spent three million pounds on an independent programme of air expansion. At an emergency meeting of the Air Board, its head, Lord Curzon, lambasted the naval members of the Board for usurping his authority. In a written letter to the full War Committee, he complained bitterly about the intransigence and interference of the Admiralty. The reply from the First Sea Lord of the Admiralty, Lord Balfour, was short and curt:

Lord Rothermere.

Gotha bomber squadron preparing for a raid on England.

The Admiralty has no intention of adapting its policy to suit the convenience of the Air Board. The Admiralty was created some generations before the Air Board and its framers had not the wit to foresee the day when it would be required to carry out its duties in subordination to another department.

The effect of this was to open a breach in the already strained relationship between the Admiralty and the Air Board. Since the onset of the war, politicians and Ministers had been toying with the idea of a separate Air Ministry and with the public now calling for retaliation for the Gotha bombing raids, it was decided to carry out a feasibility study. The man chosen for the task was General Jan Christian Smuts, a South African soldier-politician who was a *de facto* member of the War Cabinet, but with a great deal of war experience. His conclusions were that one Ministry, the Ministry of Defence, should be set up under the control of one Minister. Beneath the umbrella of this

Ministry should be three separate Ministries, the Air Ministry, the Admiralty and the War Office, each under the control of senior officers. A number of other recommendations were made with regard to separating the Admiralty and the Air Board, which culminated in the creation of the Royal Air Force some 18 months later. This is an over-simplification of the creation of the RAF, but gives some indication of the underlying causes that were instrumental in its development.

Gotha over London. The Mile End road can be clearly seen running diagonally across the bottom left hand corner of the picture.

In the reorganisation of the RNAS, squadrons were renumbered by adding 200 to the existing squadron number, eg. Naval Squadron 1 became RAF Squadron 201 and so on upwards. The five special Royal Naval Air Service officers' ranks were changed to the equivalent Army ranks by the Royal Flying Corps. However, it wasn't until after the war that the present Royal Air Force rank structure came into being. At the same time, the Women's Royal Air Force, under the command of

Lady Gertrude Crawford, who was given the rank of Chief Superintendent, came into being. In May the rank was changed to that of Commandant and the Hon. Violet Douglas-Pennant assumed command.

Major General Sir Hugh Trenchard, whose relationship with Lord Rothermere, the Secretary of State for Air, had been less than cordial from the day of his appointment, finally snapped. Rothermere, at their first meeting, was full of flattery and adulation for Trenchard, which Trenchard, a very down-to-earth person, recognised as insincerity; he realised that they were trying to use him. It transpired that Lord Rothermere and his brother Lord Northcliffe were about to carry out a campaign against Sir Douglas Haig and Sir William Robertson in an effort to get them removed. Trenchard, in exchange for his support, was to be offered the appointment of the Chief of the new Air Staff. He turned the job down in a manner which left no doubt as to where his loyalties lay.

There were numerous letters and meetings, most of them stormy, over the following three months, in which Trenchard realised that Rothermere was completely ignorant of the needs and workings of the air service. Then on 19 March things came to a head. At noon on that day, Trenchard placed a letter of resignation on Lord Rothermere's desk. Rothermere read it and immediately asked Trenchard to withdraw it. Trenchard refused and even when

SE5a fighters of 85 Squadron at St Omer on 21 June 1918. The squadron was commanded at the time by 'Mick' Mannock, who was killed a month later.

Rothermere said, 'As I am going soon myself, I would like you to withdraw your resignation now.' Trenchard refused. When asked why, he
replied, 'If you must know, I don't trust you to resign.' With that he
turned on his heels and walked away. He was succeeded by Major
General Sir Frederick Sykes and on the same day the last German airship raid to inflict casualties was carried out.

Eleven days later Lord Rothermere resigned as Secretary of State
for Air and was replaced by Sir William Weir. Weir was a good choice,
as he was an early advocate of long-range bombing and the driving
force behind the strategic air offensive launched against Germany.

The Allied Air Forces were now well in control of the skies above
the Western Front. Aircraft such as the SE5a, Sopwith Camel and the
French Spad 13 were more than a match for the German opposition.
But the Germans had quickly realised the worth of aircraft attacking
enemy ground troops and supporting their own troops from the air,
and their C Class general purpose aircraft were designed specifically
for this role. Late in 1917, the C Class type was joined by the two-seat
J Class armoured ground attack aircraft and early in 1918 by the
lighter CL Class ground attack and escort type. The theory behind
this was that it did not require fighter cover and could escort C and
J Class types. The best J Class aircraft was the biplane Junkers J1 which
was metal-covered, had a wing span of 52 feet, could fly at 96 mph and

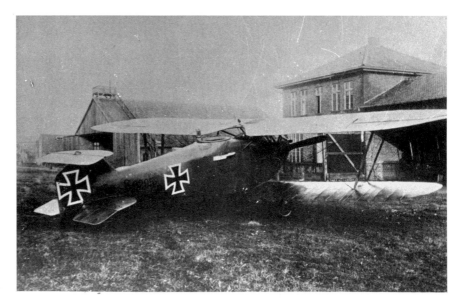

Hannover CL II.

Halberstadt CL IV. The ring in the rear cockpit is the mounting for the hand-held Parabellum machine gun.

could take considerable punishment in battle. The CL Class included the Halberstadt CL II and IV which could attain 103 mph and had three machine guns. The Hannover CL II and IIIa flew at the same speed but had two machine guns. Ahead of its time was the advanced design Junkers J 10 or CL 1, an all-metal, low-wing cantilever monoplane, used as a close-support attack aircraft.

The German High Command's plan was to launch a final series of five offensives in the spring of 1918, in a last bid to win the war. The basic strategy was to overcome the British, then turn on the French and drive for Paris. *Blitzkrieg* tactics were used to punch through the Allied lines and control of the air was essential for intelligence gathering and protective troop cover. The CI Class aircraft were ideal for this role and were renamed *Schlachstaffeln* (Battle Squadrons) and grouped in *Schlachtgeschwader*, or *Schlastas* (Battle Wings) as they were more generally known.

The signing of the peace treaty between Russia and Germany in March 1918 forced the British government to send units of the RAF to Russia to protect the northern flank against usage by the Germans. In May 1918, General Poole was sent to Murmansk as Commander of the North Russia Expeditionary Force. The RAF squadrons comprised DH4 and DH9 day bombers, Sopwith Camel fighters, Fairey, Short and Sopwith seaplanes. By this time the RAF had a total front-line strength of 2,630 aircraft, of which 1,736 were on the Western Front, 104 on the Italian Front, 41 on the Macedonian Front, 269 in the Middle East, 144 in the Mediterranean and 336 for home defence. The British aircraft industry had grown so rapidly that it produced an average of 2,668 aircraft per month in 1918. Much of this vital war work was carried out by women as most able-bodied men were in uniform. In the last six months of 1918, nearly 350,000 men and women were employed in the industry and produced 26,685 aircraft and 29,561 engines.

On 5 June 1918, Trenchard was officially appointed to command the Independent Force. He had accepted the post in May, but his appointment was held back until the politicians decided to announce it. The Independent Force was going to take the air war to the German industrial heartland by strategic bombing with the British Handley Page 0/100 bomber.

The Independent Force was the first truly independent air arm to be responsible for its operations, without interference from the ground army, although in the last stages of the war, tactical air operations were undertaken in support of the Allied armies' offensives, dropping some 220 tons of bombs on enemy airfields. The bombers

Sir Hugh Trenchard (centre) as Chief of Air Staff.

Handley Page 0/400 bomber about to land.

were based at several airfields around Nancy, comprising four day (55, 99, 104 and 110) and five night (97, 100, 115, 215 and 216) squadrons. The squadrons were equipped with Handley Page 0/100 and 0/400 bombers, DH9s and 9As. They also had one squadron of Sopwith Camel fighters to protect the bombers on daylight operations. (110 Squadron was equipped with aircraft bought by the Nizam of Hyderabad, India.)

The resumption of strategic bombing raids on Germany was in part a direct retaliation for German air raids on Britain and also designed to halt the offensive. The Handley Page 0/100 twin-engined biplane bomber first came into service in France during November 1916, and went on to become the most famous bomber of the war. Powered by two Rolls Royce Eagle II inline engines of 250hp each, it could attain a ceiling of 8,500 feet with a range of 700 miles and a maximum speed of 85 mph at sea level. With a crew of three it carried a maximum bomb load of 2,000lb, consisting of a single 1,650lb, eight 250lb bombs or three 520lb or 550lb or sixteen 112lb bombs. For defence, the bomber carried one or two Lewis machine guns on a ring mounting in the nose cockpit, one or two Lewis guns in the upper rear cockpit and a single Lewis gun mounted to fire downwards through a hole in the fuselage just behind the wings. The 100 feet span wings

Handley Page 0/400 of 214 Squadron, RAF, at Dunkirk airfield, after a night sortie in which it suffered flak damage to its wing fabric.

could be folded to enable the aircraft to fit into the canvas field hangars that were used at the time. A total of 46 Handley Page 0/100s were delivered into service.

Some months later the Handley Page 0/400 arrived. This was an improved version of the 0/100. It had a redesigned fuel system, was some 11 miles per hour faster and carried a crew of four or five – pilot, bomb aimer/front gunner, observer and one or two gunners. The 0/400 became the most widely used of the Handley Page aircraft; some 400 being delivered before the end of the war to seven RAF squadrons.

On 25 August 1918, two Handley Page 0/100 bombers of 215 Squadron, Independent Force, attacked the Badische Anilin poison gas factory at Ludwigshafen. They flew at 200 to 500 feet above the target in the precision raid and destroyed the factory. During September, the Handley Page bombers began to use 1,650lb bombs; one dropped on a factory at Kaiserlautern, reducing it to rubble. It wasn't all one-way traffic, however. On one raid that was to bomb Saarbrücken and Trier, six Handley Page bombers were brought down by anti-aircraft fire.

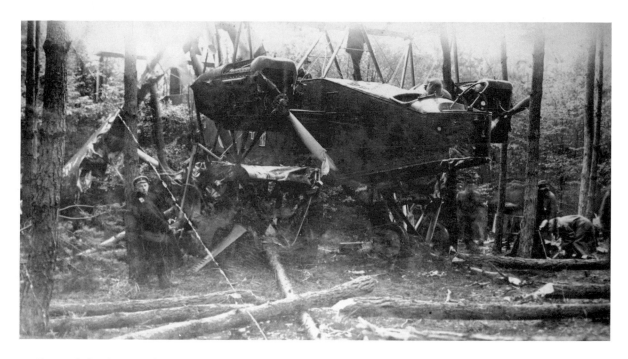

One of the last raids of the war by Zeppelins, was carried out on 5 August 1918, when early in the afternoon the L70, the latest and largest addition to the Naval Airship Division, slipped her moorings at Friedrichshafen together with the L53, L56, L63 and L65 and headed for the east coast of Britain. On board was Commander Peter Strasser, Chief of the Naval Airship Division, who was making one of his surprise trips. The airship reached the coast just after dusk and prepared to make a low-level run over Yarmouth. But unknown to them, their presence had been detected by the Leman Tail lightship. A number of British fighters were launched, among them a two-seat De Havilland DH4 flown by Major Robert Cadbury with Captain R J Leckie as his observer/gunner.

Cadbury climbed the aircraft to 16,000 feet after jettisoning a reserve tank of fuel and some of his smaller bombs. As he broke through the clouds he saw the Zeppelins just above him. Banking to the left and climbing, he turned and attacked the largest of the airships, his tracer bullets ripping a large hole through the fabric. The tracers ignited the escaping gas, the flames spreading rapidly and turning the airship into a fireball in less than a minute. The remaining airships, on seeing what had happened to the L70, turned and

A less fortunate HP 0/400 being examined by German soldiers after it had crash landed in woods near Speyer, Germany.

Peter Strasser, chief of the German Naval Airship Division.

Fregattenkapitän
Strasser

567
Postkartenvertrieb W.Sanke
BERLIN N.37.
Nachdruck wird gerichtlich verfolgt.

Lieutenants Pulling (l) and Cadbury. Cadbury was responsible for destroying the German airship L70, in which Peter Strasser died.

fled back to their base. With the demise of the L70 and the commander of the Naval Airship Division, Peter Strasser, the Zeppelin threat faded, releasing the Home Defence Squadrons to concentrate on other things.

By the end of the war the Independent Force had flown 650 missions. The five squadrons of night bombers lost 87 aircrew, killed or missing, and 148 aircraft were destroyed. The four squadrons of day bombers lost 25 aircrew, 178 missing and 58 wounded, with 103 aircraft missing and 201 wrecked in crashes. The bombers dropped about 558 tons of bombs on enemy aircraft factories, poison gas plants, steel plants and railways. Of the total, 168 tons were dropped by night and 390 by day.

In the meantime, the Germans had not been idle. Between August 1917 and February 1918, they began to transfer their large R Class 'Giant' aircraft (*Riesenflugzeug*) bombers from the Eastern Front to the Western Front to be used to raid Britain by night, escorted by Gothas.

Zeppelin-Staaken R VI.

The stripped fuselage of a Handley Page 0/400 being transported back to a German airfield for examination. Note the main petrol tank above the bomb bay cells.

The R Class bombers had been designed as long-range strategic bombing aircraft and the Zeppelin-Staaken R VI had a wing-span of 138 feet 6 inches and could carry a 2,200lb bomb load.

Eleven night raids were carried out on Britain, during which the bombers dropped single 2,200lb bombs without the loss of any R Class bombers, but inflicted heavy damage to buildings and people. The escorting Gothas, however, suffered heavy losses from defending British aircraft – notably Sopwith Camels. On the night of 19 May

1918, seven Gothas out of a total of 33 aircraft attacking London were shot down by British fighters and anti-aircraft fire, which caused the German High Command to abandon the bombing of Britain.

The Germans persevered with the giant R Class bombers and raided Paris, but again they were forced to abandon their attacks. The large bombers were too slow and vulnerable, so were switched to single tactical attacks on military targets. Towards the end of the war, the German G Class GV (*Grossflugzeug* – 'giant aircraft') developed from the AEG series and capable of carrying a 1,320lb bomb load, began to appear. But it was far too late to have any impact on the war, other than creating an interest to the Allies with regard to its size and possible potential.

The French Air Force did not appear to have any real interest in long-range bombing. The French commander, Marshal Foch, considered that the war could only be won on the ground – not in the air. Nevertheless, French bombers began to appear in 1917 in the shape of the Letord 7 three-seat reconnaissance, fighter and bomber aircraft. The twin-engined Letord 7 appeared in early 1918 and had a cannon mounted at the front of the aircraft in place of machine guns. Neither saw action.

The only large French bomber to participate in the last months of the war was the two seat Farman F50 biplane, powered by two 265hp

A Letord aircraft after a bad landing at Chatillon-sur-Seine, France, in 1918.

German airman disembarking
from a British lorry after being
captured when his Gotha was
forced down.

Lorraine engines mounted on the lower wings. Eight 165lb bombs were carried between the legs of the undercarriage, with standard machine guns mounted in the rear cockpit. Only two units were equipped with the bomber at the end of the war, although three of the bombers were flown by American squadrons. A larger French bomber – the Farman F60 Goliath – first flew in 1918 and although too late to take part in the war, did become the standard French night bomber for some years to come.

The other major Allied power to carry out strategic bombing was Italy with its large Caproni bombers. Nine months after entering the war, on 27 August 1916, the Italian Air Force began strategic air attacks on the Austro-Hungarian enemy. Their far-sighted commanders realised the potential of air power as a weapon of war, by massing large numbers of aircraft and sending them against one specific target. This was highlighted on 2 October 1918, when 56 Capronis and 142 flying boats made the last large-scale attack on the Pola Naval base, causing extensive damage and virtually putting it out of action.

Pilots of the Italian Royal Navy in fron of their Caproni Ca43 triplane bomber just before taking off on a bombing raid on Pola.

Burning wreckage of a German aircraft in Palestine, set on fire by retreating Germans.

In Palestine, the British, under the command of General Allenby, were driving the Turkish out of Palestine back towards Turkey. On 19 September 1918, a single Handley Page 0/400 bomber piloted by Captain Ross Smith, who was attached to 1 Squadron, Royal Australian Flying Corps, destroyed the Turkish telephone system at El Affule with sixteen 112lb bombs. This effectively put the Turkish communications system out of action, with the result that the next day two divisions of the Turkish Seventh and Eighth Armies, were trapped in a narrow pass – the Wadi el Fara'a – by Royal Air Force bombers of the Palestine Brigade, blocking the northern end. The trapped Turkish soldiers were systematically wiped out by British fighter and bomber aircraft.

By the end of 1918, the German Air Service had sent six *Flieger Abteilung* ('Flying Units') plus No.1(F) *Jagdstaffel* to Palestine to give air support to the Turkish army fighting the British. In the first few weeks the Germans had their fair share of aerial victories, Leutnant Kunz having three victories and Vizefeldwebel Schniedwind four. But they met their match when the entire German Expeditionary Air Force was blasted from the skies by SE5as and Nieuport 17s from 111 Squadron and Bristol fighters of 1 Squadron, Australian Flying Corps. This effectively was the end of the German air threat in Palestine.

In Macedonia, Northern Greece, the Bulgarians and Austrians opposing the British bridgehead at Salonika were assisted by *Jagdstaffeln* 25 and 28. Operating north of Salonika was 150 Squadron, RAF (formed out of flights from 17 and 47 Squadrons on 1 April 1918), flying SE5as, Bristol M1 Cs, Nieuport 17s and Sopwith Camels, whilst a detachment based at Salonika provided air defence. Fortunes were not so good along the Turkish coast for the RNAS and the Greek Air Service, who carried out the raids there. They were opposed by the German Ottoman *Feldflieger Abteilung* 6 based at Chanak, whose pilots had considerable success, especially Oberleutnant Theo Croneiss (five victories) and Leutnant Emil Meinecke (six victories). The German Air Service also sent an expeditionary force to northern Italy to assist their Austro-Hungarian allies. It was becoming increasingly obvious that in the air Germany's allies were not able to endure without help.

The German Western Front spring offensive began and the *Jagdstaffeln* were withdrawn to France. The preparations for their offensive had not gone unnoticed by the Allies and in early March the

Squadron commanders of Jagdegschwader 1 in March 1918: l-r Kurt Wusthoff, Willy Rheinhard, Manfred von Richtofen, Eric Lowenhardt and Lothar von Richthofen.

British began attacking German airfields with bombs and offensive fighter sweeps, which resulted in one of the largest air battles of the war – the Battle of Le Cateau.

In March, the Royal Flying Corps had a total of 60 squadrons on the Western Front, comprising 579 aircraft, of which 261 were fighters. The Germans had 730 aircraft, of which 326 were fighters. Despite being outnumbered, the RFC gave battle with tremendous tenacity, refusing the Germans air superiority and continuing to bomb and strafe the German lines, carrying out artillery observation flights and seeking out German fighters.

On 18 March, the British sent out 24 fighters and five bombers against the German Second Army Front and met a wall of enemy fighters, including 30 Fokker Triplanes led by Manfred von Richthofen. Five of 54 Squadron's Sopwith Camels were shot down, also two SE5as and two of the bombers. The Germans lost one Albatros.

The main German offensive against the British, on a 50-mile front, began on the morning of 21 March in a fog which prevented both sides becoming airborne. The fog cleared at noon and both sides immediately launched their aircraft, either to aid advancing German troops or to defend British troops. Most of the British fighters operated at low level, and because of this the Germans who were flying at high level did not impede the British attacks on the advancing German infantry.

However, the RFC was unable to stem the advance of the German infantry and on the afternoon of 21 March, 5 (Naval) Squadron was shelled on its airfield causing it to withdraw. Several other units had been forced to do likewise, including 84 Squadron commanded by Major Sholto-Douglas – later to become Air Marshal Sir William Sholto-Douglas during the Second World War.

The battle raged from 21 March to 28 March. On 22 March, the RFC lost 19 aircraft and the Germans 11. The German fighters still operated mostly over their own lines and the opposing Sopwith Camels who came to do battle suffered the most losses whilst attacking ground targets.

On 24 March the RFC attacked advancing German troops at Bapaume and aerial activity over the town intensified, with most of the

Oberleutnant Hermann Göring briefing pilots of JG I.

fighting being carried out at under 5,000 feet. Between Montauban and Urvilliers, the Third Army began to give way to the advancing Germans, and Major General Salmond sent the following order to the Commanding Officer of 9th Wing, Lieutenant Colonel Wilfred Freeman:

> Send out your Scout squadrons and those of 27, 25 and 62 Squadrons which are available. These squadrons will bomb and shoot everything they can see. Very low flying is essential. All risks to be taken. Urgent.

By the morning of 26 March, 37 of the 60 RFC squadrons on the Western Front were flying in crisis support of the Third Army west of Bapaume. The German offensive petered out on 28 March when the German commander, General Ludendorff, realised that it was a failure. Nevertheless, the Germans still had 2,047 aircraft facing the Allies at the end of March.

On 9 April, the Germans undertook another offensive in the Lys region but fog grounded both sides until the afternoon, when large scale aerial fighting took place. Sopwith Camels of 203 and 210 Squadrons, accompanied by SE5s of 40 Squadron, carried out strafing and bombing attacks on the advancing Germans. The RAF lost one aircraft, whilst the German Air Service lost four.

As in March, the Lys battle spread to the area between Béthune and Ypres. Seven RAF Squadrons – 1, 4 (Australian), 18, 19, 40, 203 and

Sopwith Camel flown by Lieutenant W E Cowan of 208 Squadron, being examined by German soldiers after being brought down on 16 May 1918 by Leutnant von der Marwitz of Jasta 30.

210 – attacked the advancing German forces. Four RAF and seven German aircraft were shot down – probably by ground fire, so low were they flying.

Air fighting continued until 12 April, a day which dawned fine and clear. At 0600 hours, the RAF put 137 aircraft from No.1 Brigade into the air against the still advancing enemy at Merville. Three more RAF squadrons joined the fray and fighting continued until 1900 hours, during which time 10 RAF and five German aircraft were shot down. Five German balloons were also shot down at Merville by aircraft from 210 and 40 Squadrons. This was the last day of heavy air fighting along the Lys and the German ground attack faded out on 18 April.

On 21 April 1918, Manfred von Richthofen – the top scoring ace of the war with 80 known victories – was shot down and killed in combat with Sopwith Camels of 209 Squadron. Credit for the 'kill' went at first to Captain A R Brown of 209 Squadron, but later enquiry and research put it down to 3801 Gunner Robert Buie, 53rd Battery, Australian Army, firing a Lewis machine gun. There were in fact several other claims by Australian ground gunners after it was discovered who the pilot was.

The Germans attacked again on 25 April, having once again built up a formidable air strength. Aircraft were to be used in a tactical role for the first time in an offensive ground battle. As before the attacks were thwarted and the Germans stopped.

Britain lost its highest scoring pilot on 26 July. Major Edward 'Mick' Mannock, VC, DSO and Two Bars, MC and Bar, was shot down by ground fire from the German 100th Infantry Regiment and crashed to his death behind enemy lines. His last victory was over a DFW, a few minutes before his death.

Prior to the United States of America entering the war on 6 April 1917, considerable numbers of American volunteer pilots had fought with French and British squadrons and some remained with them until the end of the war. The most successful of these volunteer pilots was Captain Edward Vernon Rickenbacker with 26 confirmed victories. On 4 March he had been posted to the 94th Aero Squadron – 'The Hat in the Ring Squadron', as it was more commonly known – commanded by Major Gervaise Raoul Lufbery. On 19 March, together with Lufbery and Lieutenant Douglas Campbell, Rickenbacker flew the first all-American patrol over German lines and ten days later gained his first victory and a DSC. Twelve months later

Rittmeister Manfred von Richthofen's funeral cortege with a guard of honour from 3 Squadron Australian Flying Corps, with rifles reversed.

Aircraft salvage and repair yard at Rang-du-Fleurs in August 1918.

he was awarded his country's highest honour – the Medal of Honor – for engaging single-handed seven enemy aircraft of which he shot down three.

On 14 April, Lieutenants Douglas Campbell and Alan Winslow of the 94th Aero Squadron flying Nieuport 28s, shot down two German aircraft, the first to fall to the United States Air Service. The French Nieuport 28 was almost exclusively used by the USAS, as 297 of them were bought by the American government as fighter aircraft. Very few were used by the French Air Service. The Nieuport 28 had unusual but effective armament – two Vickers machine guns mounted side by side on the port side fuselage, giving a deadly cone of fire.

During April, the first operational American squadrons began to arrive in time for the Battle of Aisne. It began on 27 May, when 42 German divisions attacked the French along a 25-mile front, punching their way to Château Thierry and within 56 miles of Paris by 3

Douglas Campbell of the 94th Aero Squadron Note the 'Hat in the Ring' insignia.

June. They were halted by the French and the US Second and Third Divisions.

The Americans had built up a system of air bases and flying training in France and were well prepared for battle. They had

Captain Edward V Rickenbacker, CO of 94th Aero Squadron, climbing into the cockpit of his aircraft.

reservations, however, regarding some of the aircraft, including the Nieuport 28. The Americans found that the wing fabric had a tendency to tear when the aircraft was in a dive, so they re-equipped with the French Spad S XIII, which quickly became the standard pursuit aircraft of all the USAS squadrons. It wasn't long before the first of the American pursuit groups was in action. The 1st Pursuit Group, which comprised the 27th, 94th, 95th and 147th Squadrons under the command of Major Albert M Atkinson, first went into combat on the Château Thierry sector. Their German opponents flew the Albatros D III and the Pfalz D III aircraft.

The USAS bombing and air observation squadrons, equipped with French Breguet XIVs, Salmson 2A2s and British DH4s built under licence in the United States and powered by American Liberty aero-engines, began to arrive and the pursuit groups gave protection cover.

Officers of 88th Aero Squadron at Ferme-de-Greves in August 1918, standing in front of a Salmson 2A2.

In May 1918, 145 Squadron, RAF, flying the SE5a, gave vital air support when General Allenby made his final offensive against the Turks, which ended the war in the Middle East.

During June 1918, the strength of the Royal Air Force had risen to

1,120 fighter aircraft and 422 bombers – ten of which were long range heavy bombers. The German offensive finally faltered and ended early in August, with the 1st Pursuit Group claiming 38 downed aircraft, but with the loss of 36 of their own pilots.

The German Imperial Air Service took delivery of a new fighter during August, the Fokker E V monoplane (later redesignated D VIII) and pushed it into front line service almost immediately. Within days the problem of the wing falling off reappeared, as Leutnant Rolff of *Jagdstaffel* 6 was killed when his aircraft suffered wing failure and crashed. Two days later there was another wing failure, again resulting in the death of the pilot. The remains of the aircraft were examined and the starboard wing was salvaged complete. The aircraft was withdrawn from service immediately and the remains, including the starboard wing, were sent to the Aircraft Crash Commission.

Hermann Göring, who was now commander of the *Jagdgeschwader von Richthofen*, was a personal friend of Anthony Fokker, but

Oberleutnant Ernst Udet walking away from his Fokker D VII 'Lo' during the late summer of 1918.

happened to be on leave at the time of the accidents. His deputy was Ernst Udet, who correctly went by the book and alerted the Air Crash Investigation Commission. Fokker was in trouble. He had already been before the commission on a similar problem with his aircraft, and if Göring had not been on leave it is possible that the problem would have been hushed up.

The subsequent inquiry discovered a series of defects in the manufacture of the wing, in which green wood had been used and there was insufficient glue on the joints, rendering them ineffective. The design and stress of the wing was brought into question and after a series of tests, carried out in front of Fokker and his Chief Engineer, Reinhold Platz, Fokker conceded that there were problems. He suddenly found himself under consideration for criminal proceedings to be brought against him, alleging that he had knowingly supplied defective equipment to the military. The investigation dragged on and it was only the Armistice that brought the whole sorry affair to a halt.

During the lull after the Battle of the Aisne, the 2nd Pursuit Group was formed on 29 July at Toul and was placed under the command of Major Davenport Johnson. It comprised the new 13th and 139th Squadrons and the older 103rd Squadron, which was in effect the legendary Lafayette Escadrille, now renamed and taken into the USAS.

Major William Thaw – former commander of the Lafayette Escadrille – was put in command of the newly formed 3rd Pursuit Group which comprised the 28th, 93rd, 103rd and 213th Squadrons. The 103rd and 139th Squadrons had been moved from the 2nd Pursuit Group which now consisted of the 13th, 22nd and 49th Squadrons. After many weeks of preparation the American armies, under General Pershing, launched the St Mihiel offensive on 12 September, with the USAS supporting the US 42nd Division who were in the vanguard of the battle. The USAS's 1st B Brigade commander – General 'Billy' Mitchell – gathered over 1,500 aircraft for the offensive. Opposing the USAS were the best German squadrons – including the Richthofen Circus – equipped with Fokker D VII fighters.

By 26 September the St Milhiel offensive had been won and the final Meuse Argonne push had begun. General Pershing had over 800 aircraft under his command but his now battle-hardened pilots still had to face determined opposition from the German *Jagdstaffeln.*

Camel of 41st Aero Squadron, USAS. Note the Camel insignia.

Late October saw the formation of the 4th Pursuit Group, comprising the 17th, 25th, 141st and 148th Squadrons commanded by Major Charles J Biddle. By the time the war was over, the USAS had placed 45 operational squadrons on the battlefront in just 18 months.

The United States Naval Air Arm also expanded rapidly during the war years. It had started the war with just 51 seaplanes – at the end it had 1,865. Personnel had risen from 48 officers and 292 enlisted men, to 6,716 officers and 30,696 enlisted men.

United States naval bases were established in Great Britain, France and Italy and the US Navy flew convoy and anti-submarine missions out of Le Croisic, Loire, with six 200hp French Tellier flying boats until the Armistice.

On 8 August, Allied forces launched a major offensive east of Amiens and south of the Somme. The German lines were broken by Canadian and Australian troops on a day which became known as 'The Black Day of the German Army'.

However, although the German ground forces were losing the war, the German Imperial Air Service was not losing the war in the air. On 8 May the RAF suffered its highest daily casualties of the war. The Sopwith Camel was outclassed by the 124 mph BMW-engined Fokker D VII, with which the German *Jagdstaffeln* were being equipped and a very heavy toll was taken of the Allied fighters. September 1918 was the worst month for Allied casualties since 'Bloody April' in 1917.

Fokker D VIIs under construction.

On 11 August 1918, the German Naval Division Zeppelin L53 was shot down at 18,000 feet near the Dutch coast by a Sopwith Camel fighter piloted by Sub-Lieutenant Culley using incendiary bullets. He had taken off from a flying platform constructed on top of a lighter towed by the destroyer HMS *Redoubt* at speed into the wind. The lighter used was originally built for transporting flying boats. Sub-Lieutenant Culley landed next to the *Redoubt* and was rescued, his Sopwith Camel also being recovered from the sea by crane. Culley was awarded the DSO.

The excellent French Breguet 14 two-seat tactical bomber entered service. It was powered by a 220hp Renault inline engine which gave it a speed of 121 mph and an endurance of nearly three hours with an operating height of 19,000 feet. It carried a bomb load of 520lb and an armament of up to four machine guns.

The German Naval *Seefrontstaffel* (Marine Unit) was employed in a fighter role in mid-1918, using the same aircraft as the German Imperial Air Service, to provide air cover and protection for its submarine bases on the Flanders coast. The Seaplane Flight based at Zeebrugge – commanded by Oberleutnant Friedrich Christiansen – had by 1918 gained 20 victories against the Allies and its seaplanes had carried out offensive sorties in the North Sea up to the British coastline – including attacking Ramsgate and Dover.

The British Felixstowe F2A was one of the best flying boats of the war, as was proved in an incident in June 1918 when three of the aircraft fought off 14 German aircraft which were attacking a downed F2A in the North Sea. Six of the German attackers were shot down and the remainder retreated.

Breguet 14B.2 day bomber about to land.

By the end of 1918, the German Naval Air Service had a strength of 1,130 floatplanes and 348 landplanes. Bases had been established at Heligoland, Warnemunde, Borkum, Norderney, Putzig, Sylt, Tondern, Nordholz, Barge, Wangerooge, Hage, Apenrade, Flensburg, Holtenau, Kiel, Zeebrugge and Ostende. Other fronts where bases had been established were the Dardanelles, Bosphorus, Bulgaria, Black Sea and Romania.

Opposing the German Naval Air Service on the continent were the British Royal Naval Air Service, the Belgian Air Force and French Air and Naval units. The British were the main protagonists. Their outstanding opponents were the German aces Leutnant Bertram Heinrich (12 victories), Flugmeister Gerhard Hubrich (12 victories), Oberleutnant Theodor Osterkamp (26 victories), Oberleutnant Gotthard Sachsenburg (23 victories) and Vizeflugmeister Alexandre Zenses (19 victories).

Belgium, with most of its territory overrun by the German army, did not have its own aircraft and used five Franco-British Aviation

Theodor Osterkamp with his Fokker D VIII.

Type H flying boats from a base at Calais. The French Naval Air Aeronautical Service used flying boats in preference to other types of aircraft, and by the end of 1918 it had in service 1,264 seaplanes most of which were Franco-British aviation flying boats. Maritime anti-submarine patrol bases had been established in southern France, North Africa and along the west coast of France.

Over the Western Front, the air battle still raged. On 27 October 1918, Major William George Barker of 201 Squadron, flying a Sopwith Snipe, took on in aerial combat no less than 15 Fokker D VIIs and Rumplers. Although wounded in the thigh by machine gun fire from one of the Fokkers, he continued to fight, eventually being wounded in the other thigh and elbow. Nevertheless, he shot down three of the Fokkers and forced a Rumpler C to crash-land. For this courageous action, he was awarded the Victoria Cross by King George V on 30 November 1918, to add to his DSO and Bar, MC and two Bars.

The aerial fighting continued unabated and after one particularly fierce battle on 30 October, in which the RAF lost 41 aircraft, they claimed the destruction of 67 German aircraft. The writing was on the wall for the Germans: lack of resources, fuel and experienced pilots was taking its toll, and they finally realised that they were in a hopeless situation. The Allies, on the other hand, had the might of the American industrial war machine behind them and a steady stream of reinforcements from the Commonwealth countries and the United States to support their air forces.

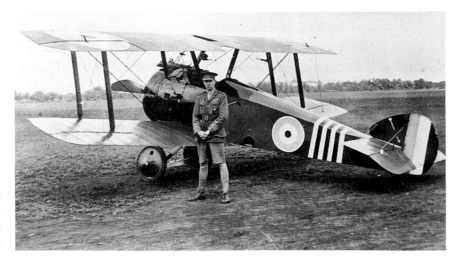

Major W G Barker VC DSO MC with Sopwith Camel No. B6313 of 139 Squadron, shortly after taking command of the squadron. Note the little Red Devil mascot at muzzle end of guns

At Bircham Newton airfield in Norfolk, England, three top secret Handley Page V/1500 bombers were standing by for the first direct air raid from England to Berlin. The V/1500 was the largest British bomber of the First World War and the first with four engines. The wing span was 126 feet, it weighed more than 12 tons – all-up weight – and was powered by four Rolls Royce 375hp engines. The V/1500 could carry thirty 250lb bombs or any multiples that did not exceed a total of 7,000lb. Before the Berlin air raid could be launched, the Armistice was signed on 11 November and the V/1500 did not see action.

Handley Page V/1500 bomber of 166 Squadron at Bircham Newton airfield.

There was one final act of defiance, however, from the German Air Service. *Jagdstaffel von Richtofen* received an order reading:

FIFTH ARMY HEADQUARTERS TO KOMMANDEUR J.G. FREIHERR VON RICHTHOFEN No.1.

YOU WILL DISARM YOUR PLANES AT ONCE AND FLY

THEM TO FRENCH AIR HEADQUARTERS AT STRASBOURG
WHERE ARRANGEMENTS HAVE BEEN MADE FOR YOU TO
LAND WITHOUT HINDRANCE. ACKNOWLEDGE.

Its commander, Hermann Göring, reacted immediately, saying
that under no circumstances was he going to allow any of his aircraft
to be handed over to the French, knowing that they had been trying
to obtain a Fokker D VIII for a long time. He informed his men of
the order and they united behind him in refusing to surrender their
aircraft to the French. Göring then decided that he would send five
of the aircraft to Strasbourg, whilst the remaining aircraft and their
pilots would fly to Darmstadt. The five aircraft took off for
Strasbourg, but with orders to destroy the aircraft on landing.
Meanwhile, the remaining members of the squadron headed towards
Darmstadt, and on landing there deliberately crashed their aircraft
beyond repair.

Members of 92 Squadron, RAF, three days after the Armistace. Major Arthur Coningham, later to become Air Marshal Sir Arthur Coningham, is seated second left, front row.

At the end of the First World War in November 1918, the Royal Air
Force was the largest air force in the world, with nearly 700 bases and
airfields, 22,647 aircraft, 27,333 officers and 263,410 other ranks.

However, although the war in Europe had ended, it still continued
in Russia. Germany and Russia had commenced peace negotiations
in 1917 to end the war between their two countries and had signed a

peace treaty in March 1918. This immediately exposed the Allies' Eastern flank to occupation by German forces.

The Imperial Russian Flying Corps – a branch of the Army – had come under the control of the Bolshevik revolutionaries and been renamed the Red Air Fleet. To counter this threat, and to aid the Tsarist regime in its civil war with the revolutionary Bolsheviks, several volunteer RAF units equipped with DH4s, DH9 day bombers, a few RE8s, Sopwith Camel fighters, Fairey III Cs, Short 184 and Sopwith seaplanes were sent to support Allied forces in north and south Russia.

In December 1918, 47 Squadron re-equipped with 12 DH9s and six Sopwith Camels and was sent to Batum, south Russia, to aid the White Russian forces. In north Russia, British troops were in position around Archangel supporting the White Russian forces. In Siberia, American, Canadian and Japanese forces were supporting General Kolchak's White Army against the Bolsheviks.

The British air contingent flew DH4s, DH9s and Short 184 seaplanes. Many well known pilots had volunteered for the Russian RAF

Lieutenants Rochford and Stone of 201 Squadron in southern Russia.

units, among them Major Geoffrey Bowman, DSO, DFC, Captain
Oliver Bryson, MC, DFC and Bar, Captain Robert Childlaw-Roberts,
MC, Lieutenant James Jones, DSO, DFC and Bar, Lieutenant Alan
Jerrard, VC, Major Keith Park, MC and Bar and Lieutenant Thomas
Williams.

Back in England on 11 January, Major General Sir Hugh
Trenchard had been reinstated as Chief of Air Staff and three days
later, on 14 January, Winston Churchill became Secretary of State for
War and Air.

The RAF contingent in Russia received several Nieuport and
Sopwith Camel fighters and in July received two Sopwith Snipes, but
there was no aerial combat on their front and they were only used in
a ground-attack role.

In April 1919, 47 Squadron, equipped with Sopwith Camels and
DH9s, was sent to south Russia to aid the White Russian forces commanded by General Denikin, whose army had no air support. The
squadron became known as A Squadron, RAF Mission, on 7 October,
1919. Towards the end of 1919, it was decided to evacuate the northern flying units and send them to south Russia to reinforce the RAF
contingent there.

The squadron was divided into three flights under the overall command of Major Raymond Collishaw. Two flights were equipped with

Russian-flown Sopwith Snipe.

DH9s and one with Sopwith Camels, under the command of Captain S M Kinkead. The south Russia Bolshevik air force was composed of a hotchpotch of German and Austro-Hungarian aircraft, plus some old French types. One Red Air Fleet pilot flew in an all-black Fokker D VII and was reputed to have 12 aerial victories against bombers of the White Russian Air Force.

Although aerial battles with the 'Reds' were infrequent, several Western Front pilots who had volunteered to fight in Russia shot down a number of Red Fleet aircraft. Kinkead brought down ten aircraft, whilst Collishaw shot down two. An American, Captain Marion Hughes Aten, shot down five 'Red' aircraft, becoming the squadron's first victor when he shot down a Nieuport Scout of the Red Air Fleet over the Volga River. He went on to account for another four aircraft – two Nieuports, one Spad and an all-black Fokker D VII – reputedly flown by the enemy's top air ace.

No.47 Squadron, RFC, carried out bombing raids on Bolshevik naval forces on the Volga River at Tsaritsyn (later Stalingrad, and now Volgograd) and claimed 17 small naval vessels sunk. The flat

Captain Sam Kinkead of B Flight, 47 Squadron, in his Sopwith Camel, southern Russia, 1919.

open Russian steppe was an ideal country for cavalry, but proved a death trap for troops caught in the open by aircraft guns and bombs. In October 1919, 221 Squadron, in co-operation with the ground army, caught a division of enemy troops advancing towards Tsaritsyn and decimated them by low-level attacks. No British aircraft were lost.

However, time was running out for the White Russians and 221 Squadron, equipped with the DH9a was taken by the seaplane carrier *Rivera* to Petrovsk, south Russia to aid the White Russian forces there. The Squadron was disbanded there on 1 September 1919. The White and other Russian forces disintegrated against the Bolsheviks, and Allied forces were evacuated in late 1919 and early 1920.

The First Air War was over and knowledge gained showed that man had developed the means of inflicting the utmost devastation on his fellow man. The reconnaissance aircraft, the fighters and the bombers of the day carried out the most terrible slaughter and damage to the enemy. Technical achievement and the development of aircraft and their weapons would continue to advance in leaps and bounds in the coming years and enable even more carnage to be reaped, this time upon innocent civilians. This knowledge gained in the formative years in the art of air warfare was priceless – but the future cost in human terms was to be horrendous.

Glossary

Ace – term to denote a pilot who had more than five victories against the enemy. A word invented by the French – originally to denote a sporting star. Not used by the British.

Abteilung – unit.

Balloon – fabric bag inflated by hydrogen gas. Either a kite balloon or barrage balloon. Kite balloon was tethered to the ground and had a basket underneath to carry an observer, who had a cable telephone link to the ground to report enemy activity. Barrage balloon was flown tethered as an anti-aircraft device.

BE – Blériot Experimental.

BEF – British Expeditionary Force.

Ceiling – the limit of an aircraft's altitude in flight.

DFW – *Deutsche Flugzeug-Werke* (German aircraft manufacturer).

DH – De Havilland

Escadrille – French term for squadron.

FE – Fighter Experimental.

Feldfliegerabteilung – German field aviation unit.

Flechettes – small steel darts dropped from an aircraft on to troops.

Flieger Abteilung – German flying unit.

Freiherr – baron.

Hun – German personnel. Word used by the British.

Jasta – abbreviation for *Jagdstaffel* (qv).

Jagdgeschwader (JG) – German fighter group.

Jagdstaffel – German fighter squadron.

Kampfgeschwader (KG) – German bombing unit.

Kanone (Ace) – German pilot with ten aerial victories

Liberty engine – American 12-cylinder water cooled aero engine developed in 1917 after the United States entered the war.

Luftschiff – airship.

LZ (*Luftschiff Zeppelin*) – Zeppelin airship.

LVG – *Luft-Verkehrs Gesellschaft* (German aircraft manufacturer).

Nacelle – part of the aircraft fuselage or wing which accommodates airscrew.

Ordre Pour Le Mérite – German decoration also known as the 'Blue Max'.

RAF – Royal Air Force

RE – Reconnaissance Experimental

RFC – Royal Flying Corps.

Rittmeister – cavalry captain.

RN – Royal Navy.

RNAS – Royal Naval Air Service.

RNVR – Royal Naval Volunteer Reserve.

SE – Santos Experimental

Schlachstaffeln – German battle squadrons.

Schlachtgeschwader – German battle wings.

Schlastas – abbreviation for *Schlachtgeschwader* (qv).

USAS – United States Air Service.

Bibiliography

Bickers, R T , *The First Great Air War,* Hodder & Stoughton, 1988.

Bowyer, C, *Albert Ball VC,* William Kimber, 1977.

Boyle, A, *Trenchard,* Collins, 1962.

Bruce, J, *The Aeroplanes of the RFC (Military Wing),* Putnam, 1982.

Christienne, C, & Lissarague, P, *French Military Aviation,* Smithsonian, 1986.

Fredette, R, *The Sky on Fire,* Harvest, 1966.

Grey & Thetford, *German Aircraft of the First World War,* Putnam, 1962.

Jablonski, *The Knighted Skies,* Nelson, 1964.

Rawlinson, A, *The Defence of London,* Harvest, 1918.

Treadwell, T C, *Submarines with Wings,* Conway, 1985.

Weyl, A R, *Fokker – The Creative Years,* Putnam, 1961.

White, C M, *The Gotha Summer,* Hale, 1986.

Index